THE LAST SUMMER OUR
CHILDHOOD

Written by
Margueritte A. Brown

Dewilda Williams, Editor

ISBN 1-886493-10-3
Papercover
Library of Congress Catalog Card Number: 95-072928

Above Success is God!

Published by

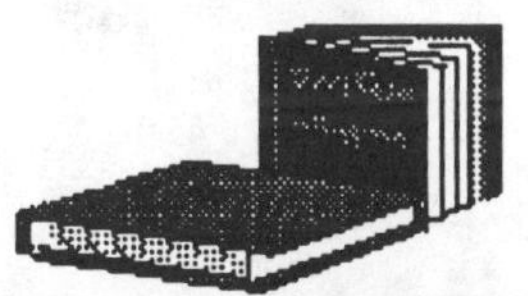

NBC Study Publishing Co.
P. O. Box 55444
Tulsa, OK 74155-0444

Dedicated to

Sharon, Mary, and Delores
for their "You can do it, girl" attitude

and to
My baby, Bruzzie
who left all too soon

and
special thanks to our precious H.S.,
for His eternal inspiration

THE LAST SUMMER OF OUR CHILDHOOD

**Written by
Margueritte A. Brown**

Table of Contents

THE LAST SUMMER OF OUR CHILDHOOD

by
Margueritte A. Brown

THE LAST SUMMER OF OUR CHILDHOOD

By
Margueritte A. Brown

The year was 1937. A year when history recorded such events as the explosion of the Hindenburg dirigible; when the "Dust Bowl" was a stark reality in the southwestern United States; hundreds of thousands of families moved to California seeking a better life; and ---- doctors still made house calls!

In the spring of that year the Andy Hall family also turned their thoughts toward the west, but not because of the Dust Bowl, or any other world shaking event. The Hall family's decision was based solely on the fact that Big Andy's unexpected death has left his wife, Addie, to raise their six children alone.

THE LAST SUMMER OF OUR CHILDHOOD introduces us to a then major entity in society. Simply, **A FAMILY.** Stroll gently through the summer following Big Andy's demise with the "Walking" Halls as they grieve, cope, then adjust. Share with Marlee the bewilderment of a ten-year old girl when she hears her beloved daddy shout from his sick bed, "The chariots are coming for me!".

Meet and dream with Grandma Maybelle, who loves "L.A." (as she fondly calls Los Angeles), and muses, "why don't they call El Paso 'E.P.'?".

Sympathize with Little Andy as he agonizes between loyalty to the family and his own desire to go away to college; and Addie's heart-wrenching decision to sell the family home.

Laugh with and at; five year-old Ben when he gets his head stuck between the pickets of the front yard fence; Marlee's imitation of Grandma playing cards with her society L.A., friends; and at thirteen year-old Jack as he and Marlee's twin brother, Mark, take a forbidden, but exhilarating downhill ride in Marlee's dollbuggy that ends as a comical misadventure.

Our memory is rekindled at the bitter-sweet love between sixteen year-old Vivian and her high school sweetheart, Joshua. Inescapably, we shed silent tears as the family bids farewell to their home, relatives and friends as Little Andy boards a southbound train for college in Austin, and the rest of the family head westward to the City of Angels to begin a new and different life.

GOIN' HOME

CHAPTER ONE

It was the first warm Saturday of spring, eight years after the beginning of "The Great Depression". Most of America's southwestern states still labored under the burden of that depression as well as a drought. Being poor already, the depression had little or no visible effect on the four cinnamon skinned children engaged in a game of marbles on the ground of their grassless front yard. Throughout their young lives their daddy had been fortunate to have always worked as a porter at the train Depot. For that reason, they were only vaguely aware that there was a depression at all.

The mood of the three boys and their sister appeared, on the surface, in contrast to the brooding overhead clouds. Clouds that held little promise of much needed precipitation in this dry west Texas border town. Infrequent rain during the last few years, coupled with the fact that small feet tramped down every tiny green blade that poked itself through the ground, caused most of the families in El Paso with children to have long since given up the struggle to maintain the luxury of a lawn and settle for a few flowers inside the fenced yards.

The boys conversed between themselves with such remarks as, "bet you can't hit that one," or "who taught you how to play marbles," and howls of laughter erupted whenever one of them missed a shot, but the thin ten year old girl, squatting with her dress tucked loosely between her legs, squinted her dark almond-shaped eyes and stared thoughtfully at the ground. In one hand she held a marble, and the index finger of her other hand aimlessly twisted one of the long thick braids that hung halfway to her waist. As she shifted her weight, she also shifted her train of thoughts momentarily. The hem of her dress slid from its protected position between her knees and dusted the Texas clay-dirt. Marlee Hall vowed silently, as she did each time that she played marbles with her brothers, *when I get grown I'm gonna wear pants anytime I want to, even if Mama did say "nice girls don't wear pants."*

"Your shot, Marlee," Jack commanded, a hint of irritation in his tone. At fourteen, Jack's former adolescent tenor voice had changed to a deep baritone. "Are you daydreaming again?"

Startled, Marlee's attention was drawn back to the present. "I wasn't daydreaming. I was thinking."

"Thinking?" The corners of Jack's mouth curled in an almost unperceptive leer. "I just bet you were. Thinking, or daydreaming, you can't play if you don't keep your mind on the game." "I can play anytime I want to," she replied tartly, cutting her eyes at her older brother. "<u>You're</u> not the boss."

"Leave her alone, Jack," Mark cautioned. His voice softened as he turned to his twin sister, "Go on Sis, take your turn."

Mark was four years younger than Jack, but the two brothers physical appearance was more alike than was that of the twins. Both boys resembled their father whose fine chiseled features were unquestionably Sudanese, African. Their skin was like polished leather pulled tight over high cheek bones. Deep set dark eyes evenly located above a wide nose were in direct contradiction to the thin lips that revealed straight white teeth when drawn back in a smile.

Unlike Jack, the younger boy was not much of a talker, which caused the rest of the family to consider his occasional discourses with a certain amount of seriousness. Jack on the other hand, was quick of speech, impatient, and oft times hyper-critical.

Marlee, although thin and gangly of body, bore a striking resemblance to her mama. She had thick, long kinky hair, large dark eyes shaped like two almonds covered with lush thick lashes, smooth round cheeks and full lips. Her skin was the color of creamy chocolate. Her zest for life was infectious and she, even at ten years old, was fierce about her loves and loyalties.

Marlee tightened her skirt around her thighs, got down on one knee, took her shot, then resumed her squatting position and settled back into reflection. She couldn't seem to shake the feeling of...sadness. No, that wasn't it. She wasn't sad, exactly. More like apprehension, like waiting for something to happen and not knowing just what, or why. Her thoughts turned, as did her eyes, to the house, and her daddy, and her mama.

Big Andy Hall had been sick in bed for over three weeks, with what their mama said was "a real bad cold that was trying to turn into pneumonia." From what Marlee could see, the "trying" was over. Daddy <u>had</u> pneumonia! And poor Mama. Looking so tired lately as she literally ran to Daddy's bedside every time he had a coughing spell--to cover him up, give him some of the medicine that Dr. Rivers had left, or help him sit up so that he could catch his breath. And the other times when Mama had to help Daddy out of bed so that he could use the slop-jar because he seemed too weak to make it down the hall to the toilet.

"Daddy's gonna be alright, ain't he?" Marlee burst out, looking helplessly from one brother to the other. "Sure he is," Mark comforted her. "Now don't you be worrying about Daddy?" "He don't look so good. And you know how weak he is." "Take my word for it," Mark reassured her. "Daddy is gonna pull out of this sickness any day now. He don't look good 'cause he haven't been eating much lately. You'd look bad too, if you was only eating soup." "I guess so. But..." "No 'butts'. Daddy is gonna be fine. Right Jack?"

Jack managed a weak smile before lowering his eyes to the circle of marbles on the ground. Inside himself he wasn't so sure, but he couldn't let the others see any doubt in him. Five year-old Ben, who had been quietly absorbing the conversation, now looked from face to face. His childish mind was puzzled, but no one asked him what he thought.

The Hall children were not allowed to play outside of the yard anymore without permission from their parents. Only Little Andy and Vivian were exempt because they were in high school, but Missouri Street was off-limits to the other four children. When Big Andy married Addie nineteen years ago, they were lucky if three automobiles passed down their street in a day, but now there were many vehicles, and some traveled as fast as twenty miles an hour. A child running into the street chasing a ball could get hit if the driver failed to see them and stop. Who would have imagined that a child playing in the street might be in danger of something else besides an automobile. A harmless BICYCLE!

It all happened one day when Marlee was four years old. Late one summer afternoon, for some unknown reason, Marlee decided to go out of the unlatched gate to meet her daddy, who rode a bicycle to and from work. Up until that point, she had never ventured outside the yard without one of her parents, and the gate was always kept latched to prevent any such occurrence.

Big Andy had begun to slow down as he approached his house, and had looked over his shoulder to wave at a neighbor. At the same time, chubby Marlee ran out of the gate and headed down the sidewalk straight toward Big Andy, who by now had left the street, and was riding on the sidewalk. As he turned his head back around he saw his baby daughter. Her face glowed with childlike expectancy as her tiny feet propelled her toward him.

Realizing that they were on a collision course, he shouted, "MARLEE, STOP!" while turning the handlebar sharply to the left and furiously back-peddling in an attempt to avoid running her down. His effort succeeded, almost, but not before he grazed her, knocking her to the pavement, and him__along with the bicycle__against the fence. Scrambling to untangle his long legs from the bicycle he sprang up and bounded the short distance to his daughter, who was sprawled on the sidewalk, shrieking at the top of her lungs. A quick inspection of the child showed no visible injury, except a scratch on her lower right leg and dirt from the sidewalk extending from her legs to the thick braids on her head. Gathering her into his arms, Big Andy could not speak because of the overwhelming feeling of relief that his baby had not been seriously injured.

The bicycle lay forgotten as he tenderly carried his crying child through the open gate, up the walk, and deposited her on the bottom step of the front porch.

The noise had brought her mama to the door with an inquiring, "Marlee, what's wrong with you, child?" Then seeing her husband, she asked with concern, "Honey, what happened?"

Big Andy was so unnerved by the accident, and the thought of what could have happened, simply shook his head and looked at his Marlee, whose loud crying had tapered to heaving sobs. Then, upon seeing her mama the little girl ran up the steps, clutched the woman's leg, and buried her head in Addie's apron. "Daddy...ran over...Me!" she managed between sobs.

Addie gave her husband a quizzical look. Big Andy pointed toward the open gate. Then the expression on his face slowly changed from distress to anger. The gate latch was <u>UP.</u> One of the older children must have left the gate unlatched!

"Marlee," Addie said, her tone gentle but firm. "Marlee Hall. Stop crying now, baby. You're not hurt, just scared. Daddy didn't mean to knock you down. You shouldn't have been outside the yard, you know." She brushed the dirt off of the child's dress and hair, and with the corner of her apron wiped Marlee's tear stained face.   After kissing her on the cheek, Addie turned the girl around toward Big Andy. "Go on now, why don't you, and give Daddy a big hug? He feels bad too, you know."

Marlee obediently trotted over to Big Andy, who had sat down on the steps. Easing her tiny body onto her daddy's lap she circled his neck with her arms. Big Andy held her close for a long time, even after Addie went back into the house.

Later that evening after supper, while all the family was still sitting at the table, Big Andy had a serious talk with his children.

"I ain't gonna ask who lef de gate unlatched, tho ah got mah 'spicions," he said, pushing his chair back and slowly rising from the table. The kitchen became instantly quiet except for Addie's feet upon the linoleum as she discreetly cleared the table of dinner dishes.

Big Andy's face was stony. His voice had an ominous tone as he continued, "But, from dis day on, I promises ya," he paused and gave, one by one, a piercing look at each of the children, "If'n any of yawl under twelve go out de yawd widout p'mission from ya mama or me, 'ceptin when ya goin to school...ya gonna git a taste o' mah leather strap like ya never had b'fo. Y'understan me?" They all nodded their heads in silent accent, being too afraid to utter a sound. It was a rare occasion to see Big Andy so provoked and displeased with his children. Ordinarily bad behavior merited a simple whipping, but very rarely this kind of lecture.

At this point he looked directly at his oldest son, Little Andy. "Jes so's ya won't think ah'm showin favorits, ya ole'r ones___if ya fo'gits to latch dah gate___ya gon git some o' dah same, b'leeve me."

Marlee was ten now, and from that day to this she stayed inside the yard and waited for her daddy to come home from work.

Mark frowned as he too thought of his family. Casting a secretive glance at Marlee, he thought, *It's funny that Marlee was the only one to put into words what we all are probably thinking, because the whole family seems to be in a strange mood today. It's like we are all waiting for something to happen, and hoping that it won't.* Shrugging his shoulders he concluded, *It's probably just my imagination, or maybe the weather or something.* With that he turned his attention back to the game.

"Vivian! Viv...yann!" Addie's voice pierced the still air. Her small frame appeared even smaller as she leaned wearily against the front screen door.

"She's not out here, Mama!" Jack shouted back.

"'She's not out here'?" Addie demanded as she pushed open the screen and came out onto the porch. Extending her hand backward in an unconscious motion she caught the screen before it slammed shut. "What do you mean 'she's not out here'? Where is she?"

"She went down the street to Mrs. Dullums' house." Marlee answered. Vivian spent every minute she could at the Dullums' house and Marlee was always having to make excuses for her when Mama found out.

"More like Joshua Dullums than Mrs. Dullums," Jack snickered under his breath.

"You shut-up Jackson Hall. Are you trying to get Viv in trouble?" Mark hissed through his teeth. Jack glared at his brother and would have pushed him backward had not Addie given them both a stern look. He and Mark usually got along very well, except when Mark called him "Jack-son". He wished that he had been named after his daddy. Daddy was the kind of man that he wanted to be like when he grew up. To be called Jackson implied that he was the son of Jack. Even though Big Andy had assured him more than once that it didn't matter what his name was..."you's mah son, an'll always be mah son. Ya mama 'n me only named yah Jackson count of that was mah papa's name." Still, he hated to be called Jackson.

"Jack, run down to Mrs. Dullums and tell your sister she had best get herself home quick. And I do mean quick. I declare, Vivian is never around when I need her," Addie commanded. Exasperation, coupled with weariness, almost overwhelmed her. She blinked her eyes several times and hoped that her eyeglasses hid the tears that hovered on the brink of her eyelids.

"She said she would be right back, Mama," Marlee pleaded, even though she was sure that her older sister wouldn't. The children all knew that when Vivian slipped off to see Joshua it was no telling when she might come home.

"Don't make excuses for her, Marlee." Addie knew why Vivian spent all her time at the Dullums' house. "And who gave her permission to leave anyway? Just because she's sixteen don't mean she's grown. It's times like this that I wish I'd agreed with your daddy when he wanted to get a telephone. Now I really need one. Oh well, no use crying over spilled milk. I'll just have to wait until Vivian gets back." "Let me help Mama. I can do whatever you wanted Viv to do."

"I don't know, Marlee," Addie replied with some hesitation. "You're so young. I'm not sure you could...I don't know. I really need her to go down the block to Mrs. Tate's to use her telephone to call Dr. Rivers." "Dr. Rivers? For Daddy? Is Daddy worse?" Blurted out Mark, jumping up from where he had gone to sit on the porch steps.

The shocked sound in his voice caused Addie to pause before answering. In the most matter-of-fact tone that she could manage she said, "Daddy's a little restless, that's all. I want Dr. Rivers to come and give him something so he can sleep." *No sense alarming the children unduly*, she thought, but her insides were in turmoil. Big Andy had symptoms that she had seen before, and she was scared. Bad symptoms. "Tell you what, Marlee, you go in and sit with Daddy 'til I get back. I'll go call the doctor myself. Now mind you, don't let him throw the covers off. I don't want him to catch more cold than he's already got. If he gets too restless or needs to use the pottie, call Mark."
"I will Mama. I'll see to him real good."

"I know you will, child," Addie patted Marlee on the shoulder reassuringly. Then turning to Mark, she commanded, "When Miss Vivian gets home you tell her that I'll take care of her later," then pointing a threatening finger at the children, "and don't you all leave this yard, do you hear me?"

By the time Addie finished closing the gate Marlee was pulling her chair up to the side of her daddy's bed, preparing to 'sit' with him until her mama's return.

Andy Hall was not called Big Andy just because he was the father of Andy Jr., but because he was in fact a big man. He stood over six feet and weighed well over two hundred pounds. By the time he reached sixteen he had attained his full height, which worked to his advantage because by the age of ten he had lost both mother and father.

Before the turn of the century, and for many years afterward, there were no orphan asylums for colored children. If an orphaned child were lucky a relative would take them in, but Big Andy was an only child born of parents who were former slaves in Southern Georgia. After the Emancipation, his father left the area where he had been enslaved. Because the older man could not read or write he lost track of his blood relatives who had been with him on the plantation. When Jackson, Big Andy's father, died in an accident, the young boy was literally on his own. His mother Margaret, had died giving birth to baby Andy. Big Andy survived by working at various farms for his board and keep. Since he was big for his age, and a hard worker, he had no problem getting work.

Because he worked most of his young life, Big Andy had very little schooling, but he was quick to learn. When he reached eighteen he decided to head west where he could get a "real" job. He had heard that in Texas strong men could get work as "roustabouts" for the railroad, so Big Andy left Georgia and ended up in El Paso where he got a job loading railroad freight cars. After several years he was promoted to Redcap, as the depot porters were called.

He didn't make as much money as he had as a roustabout, but he didn't have to work as hard. This fact enabled him to hold down two jobs. The Porter job in the day, and cleaning office buildings in the night.

There had not been a lot of women in Big Andy's life before that Christmas day in 1916, but from the minute that Leon Samuels introduced him to the Samuels family, Leon's youngest daughter became Big Andy's present and forever future.

Andrew Hall fell unredeemably in love with everything about Addie Samuels. The way she tilted her head back when she laughed, revealing even white teeth behind her full lips, and her gentle dark eyes that sparkled with the joy of life. The way she wore her long frizzy black hair in a thick braid that was wound around her head, resembling a crown. He loved the sound of her quick, deliberate steps as she moved about the house, helping her mama prepare Christmas dinner, and most of all, the way he felt when she stood near him later that evening as they sang carols in the neighborhood. Her head barely reached his shoulder. He marveled at the difference between Addie and her tall, aloft older sister, Hettie.

When he was sure that Addie felt the same way about him he asked for her hand in marriage. A marriage that had brought immeasurable happiness and six precious children in the last eighteen years.

Big Andy's deepest regret during those years was that, because of the necessity of working two jobs, his only real time with his children was on Sundays.

Sunday was their day together. The first thing in the morning after they washed up they ate a hearty breakfast of biscuits, grits, sausage and gravy. Then they walked to Second Baptist Church on Second and Virginia streets for services. When the weather was nice__not too hot or windy__ they would return home the long way, going westward up Second to Mesa street, then north on Mesa through the business part of town, which was usually deserted except for a few other strollers. Then they would relax for a while at the Old San Jacinto Plaza, then on to Missouri street and home.

After dinner, which Addie always prepared on Saturday, Big Andy and his children played baseball in the back yard, which was as devoid of grass as the front.

As with many of the other yards, there was a neat flower bed running the length of the south fence. This was Addie's pride and joy, next to her children. Big Andy always found time through the years to dig up the sod, turning ashes taken from the stove into the dirt to sweeten it, and then raking the soil back and forth until it was ready for Addie's flowers. He derived a great deal of pleasure and satisfaction doing special little things like preparing the flower bed for his wife.

But today, Big Andy was unable to do **anything** for Addie, or his children. Today he lay in the big old brass bed, his large body made vulnerable and at the mercy of___Double Pneumonia!

Marlee patiently covered him once more, trying to make him comfortable. "Can I get you something, Daddy? Do you want a drink of water or something?" Big Andy showed no sign of hearing his daughter. Instead, his restlessness became aggravated. Rolling his head from side to side on the pillow, he brushed his large calloused hand across his damp forehead. Once more he pushed the cover away. A low mucous-filled gurgle resonated from his lungs as he labored to breath. Perspiration dripped from ever pore in his body.   Abruptly, before Marlee could retrieve the blanket, he sat bolt upright in the bed. With one hand raised as though to stop some unseen force, he lifted his eyes toward the ceiling and shouted hoarsely, **"They's coming after me! The chariots they be coming after me! Oh Lord! they's coming!"**

Falling back on the pillow with a great shutter his body went limp as his precious life began it's final exit from Big Andy Hall.

Marlee's eyes were as big as two brown saucers as she stood riveted to the floor beside the bed. Her mouth opened and closed several times but no sound came out. Thoughts came and went in her head. She had the sensation of being two different people. One standing petrified beside her daddy's bed, and the other one over in the corner watching in disbelief and denial, looking at her and her daddy. Here and there. Two Marlees'!

Just then Addie entered the room, her worst fears realized. Before she saw it, she sensed death in the room. Then, seeing Marlee, she acted purely by instinct. Without a word she swiftly grasped the young girl by the shoulders and propelled her out of the room, through the parlor, and onto the front porch. "Stay here!" Addie commanded, and turning, she retreated into the house to face what she must.

Marlee remained where her mama had left her, her wide eyes staring blankly out to nowhere.

Slowly thoughts began to stir in her mind. Memories of a more bearable time. Happy memories, yet strange feelings.

Happy memories like last summer when her and mama and the other children went on the train to Corpus Christi for a visit with great-aunt Madge. The trip had not cost them anything because Daddy worked for the railroad, and his family got passes each year. Aunt Madge was Grandma Samuels's sister, and she lived in a big old house in a nice part of town. Mama said that Aunt Madge really knew how to live (what ever that meant). Anyway, Aunt Madge had taken all of the family for their first trip to the seashore where they enjoyed the thrill of splashing in the warm gulf waters. Marlee didn't know there was so much water in the world. It just went on and on as far as one could see.

The four boys had ventured as far into the surf as their waists, with Marlee following close behind. But not Vivian. Vivian would never risk getting her long thick black hair wet, especially since it took her more than an hour each day to curl it. So after the initial thrill of getting her feet wet she had retreated to the beach's dry sand, to sit on the blanket with Mama and Aunt Madge, to see, and be seen. Not so with Marlee. Her hair was something that was more Mama's concern than hers. She just wanted to go into the water with her brothers, so she happily followed her brothers as they explored the water further and further from the shore. Addie, who had been watching, brought Marlee's adventure to an abrupt halt.

"Marlee!" Addie called. "Marlee! You're going out too far. Come on back!"

Marlee turned and gave her mama a pleading look. "Oh, Mama, please. I'll be careful," she shouted back.   "NOW MARLEE!"

Although she was usually an obedient child, she had been tempted to keep going and pretend that she hadn't understood what her mama had said. But habit won out. So with tears and a face that said "I wish I was a boy," Marlee had bit her lip and splashed angrily back to shore.

Seeing such disappointment on the child's face, Addie added, "Go build yourself a castle in the sand, why don't you?"

The small girl had not wanted to build a sand castle. She wanted to play with her brothers. Obediently she sat down in the shallow water where the warm surf covered her legs. As each wave rolled in, the water splashed up to her chest. But, as the water receded she had experienced the strangest sensation. She felt as though she were being pulled out to sea___ yet she never moved.

That was the way that she felt now as she stood on the porch, alone and confused. Wave after wave washed over her, threatening to engulf her, unmercifully pulling her closer to the reality of what was happening. The chariots were coming...to take her daddy away!

A short time later, after Marlee went into the house to sit with Big Andy, Jack returned, breathless from running several blocks down to Joshua's and back. He felt a twinge of guilt that he had not looked any further than the front porch of the Dullums's house for his sister. That was where Vivian and Joshua usually visited. Guilty because deep down inside he was glad that he had not found her. When Vivian left the house without permission, she was never punished as severely as Jack or Mark were, but he was sure that she would "get it" this time.

"Is Mama back yet?" Jack panted, directing his inquiry at Mark, who was sitting on the front steps with Ben.

"Not yet. Want to play some more marbles?"

"Mm. I don't think so," Jack replied, glancing toward the front door. "It's no fun. I mean, just the two of us."

"What about me? I can play!" Ben's feelings were hurt.

"I'm sorry, little guy," Jack apologized. "I meant 'the three of us'." He grinned and rubbed Ben's head playfully. *It really isn't much fun without___I hate to admit it___Marlee.*

"I wish Little Andy didn't have to work today," Mark sulked. "He could play some touch football with us if we could get Joshua, too."

"If wishes were horses, beggars would ride," Jack said. "So stop wishing. Anyway, he's just taking Daddy's place until Daddy can go back to work. Let's go in the back yard and make something." Beckoning to Ben he said, "Come on, little guy. We can't leave you out here alone. Mama would skin us alive."

There were a lot of things in the backyard that they could make something out of if they used their imagination. A huge pile of wood; some discarded tires that had been retrieved from a neighbor who owned an automobile; some rope, and last years battered red wagon.

"I know what we can do," proclaimed Jack. "We can take the wheels off of the wagon and make a scooter."   "A   scooter! Yeah, that's a good idea," replied Mark in agreement. "Yeah, that's a good idea," mimicked Ben.

Retreating to the backyard, the trio went about disassembling the wagon with enthusiasm. The task was almost completed when suddenly, from the front, they heard Marlee shrieking at the top of her lungs. "Mark! Mark! It's Daddy!"

Mark, with Jack and Ben close behind, dropped the wagon and wrenches, and raced around the side of the house. The sight that greeted them brought the three boys to an abrupt halt at the foot of the porch.

There stood Marlee. Utter distress blanketed the face of the thin distraught figure. Her eyes were like giant marbles swimming in a pool of tears. Both of her small brown hands were clasped over her ears in a vain attempt to shut out the sound of her own words.

Upon seeing Mark, the young girl leaned slightly toward her twin brother for comfort as convulsing sobs racked her total being. **"Oh Mark! Daddy is dying! Our...Daddy...is dying!"**

GRANDMA MAYBELLE

CHAPTER TWO

Addie's mother, Maybelle Samuels, arrived two days after Big Andy's death, and immediately took charge of the children, who were excused from school until after the funeral. She saw to it that they ate - which, for the first time in their lives, they had to be coaxed to do - and made sure that Ben and Marlee got their hair combed. Outside chores were assigned to the four younger children to keep them occupied, but as soon as they finished they came back into the house and sat around the kitchen table, looking like lost sheep.

"Go on outside and play, children," Maybelle said, with obvious sympathy. "No use sitting in the house looking sorrowful. Your daddy wouldn't want that."

"We don't feel much like playing, Grandma," Marlee answered in a pitiful whisper.

"Where is Daddy gone, Grandma? Will he be back soon?" Ben asked in bewilderment. "Why does Mama keep crying?"

Taking the small boy up in her arms, Maybelle tried to explain. "Your daddy is gone to heaven to live with Jesus. Your mama is just kinda sad that he's gone, but you mustn't worry about it. I'm sure that your daddy is happy up there in heaven, and one day we'll all see him again." She spoke more to herself than to Ben. Putting the boy down, she said, "Now go on outside like good children, for grandma."

Ben could not understand why his daddy would want to go away to heaven, or any where else, without him, or Mama.

Grandma went out of the room, so he followed the others out back, pondering the whole thing in his young head.

For the next few days, between Big Andy's death and his funeral, a steady stream of relatives, neighbors, and friends came to the house on Missouri street. Along with their condolences they brought cakes, pies, crisp fried chicken, baked ham, a variety of breads, and who-knew-what else.   The coffee pot on the big old wood-burning stove was never allowed to become empty. One of the neighbor women appointed herself unofficial dishwasher, and several of the church sisters busied themselves around the house each day with sweeping, making beds, and generally keeping things clean and in order.

Whenever Addie attempted to do some chore she was gently escorted back into the parlor with a kind, "Don't you fret yourself, honey. We've got everything under control."

The mourners kept their voices' low, barely above a whisper, to - as was the custom - show reverence to the dead. Big Andy could not have heard them now even if they were screaming at the top of their lungs. Screaming was what Addie felt like doing, in the still of the night, after all the visitors were gone and her family was, she hoped, asleep.

She moved about like a sleepwalker during the daytime. It wasn't that she was in shock. Or, *maybe I am*, she thought. *But I have to hold up for the children's sake.* Each morning when she opened her eyes she set her mind on a sort of track, and with eyes straight ahead, she followed that track throughout the day. It was only in the deep, black night that she let herself get off that track, bury her head in the pillow and scream, cry, call out to Big Andy, and cry some more. The pain around her heart was like a vise, squeezing tighter and tighter. One night she actually thought of just letting go, and joining Big Andy. Then she remembered her children, and fought to hold on through one more night. She was glad that Marlee had gone to sleep on a cot in the room with Vivian and Grandma.

Little Andy (who at seventeen was far from little) became just plain "Andy." Some of the older folks even referred to him as "the man of the house, now." Andy was too deep in grief to take in the full meaning of the words. He didn't mind working in his daddy's place at the Depot, but he had no desire to take Big Andy's place as man of the house. Not now. Not ever. He just wished that his daddy were still alive.

Vivian spent most of the time during those next days alternating between crying, and re-making up her face. After the shock of coming home to find out that Daddy had died began to wear off, guilt was added to her grief. She found it hard to stay in the house with so many people wandering in and out of the rooms, so she asked permission to go out to east El Paso to Aunt Hettie's house. She had to be alone for a few hours, to try to sort out her feelings. At the very time that her mama had needed her the most___she and Joshua were sitting in the swing out in his backyard, holding hands and stealing quick, furtive kisses.

Vivian walked down Missouri street, slowly, putting one foot in front of the other, her eyes seeing only the sidewalk, and the image of her daddy___and Joshua.

Joshua was her first boyfriend, and she really loved him. Addie said that Vivian's so-called love was nothing more than infatuation, but she stoutly contented that it wasn't. She even wanted to get married next year when they graduated. Joshua wanted them to get married too___but not until he finished college!

"But Josh," she had said to him that fateful morning. "I admire you for what you want to do. Really I do. Go to college and whatnot. All I ask is that you try to see my side." At this point she had softly stroked his face with the back of her hand. "I figured," she continued, "that after graduation we could move to Los Angeles, and live with my grandma until we could save enough money to get our own place. I'm sure that you could get a good job there. Grandma wrote Mama that there are all kinds of jobs to be had by a young Negro man. The son of one of her friends drives for a famous movie star."

"I don't know that I want to live in California, sweetheart," he frowned. Vivian was one of the prettiest girls he had ever known, with her thick ebony hair, keen features, and slender, well-proportioned body. He wanted nothing more than to spent the rest of his life with her, but, <u>not in California!</u> "Besides," he had said, "what about my Mama? I couldn't leave her."

Joshua's mama! Vivian had thought ruefully. *I had forgotten about <u>her</u>. But I can't get into <u>that</u> subject right now. I've got to get back home before Mama misses me. I'm sure that I can change his mind before graduation next year. There's plenty of time.* At least she had thought that there was plenty of time.

"One year is long enough to wait, but five years! I'm not sure that I can wait that long, darling," Vivian had murmured, as she leaned over and kissed him on his forehead. Confident that she had made her point, she left.

Walking briskly toward home, she had hummed softly to herself with a feeling of satisfaction. If there was one thing that she was sure of, it was how Joshua felt about her.

The minute that she walked through the gate she had been gripped with a strange uneasy feeling that something was wrong. In the first place, she neither saw, nor heard the boys, or her sister playing in the yard. They wouldn't all be inside the house this time of day, especially since she had left them playing marbles less than a half hour. Or was it___an hour ago?

Vivian had decided to go around the house and enter through the back door, hoping that Addie would be in the bedroom with Big Andy. If not, then perhaps the older woman would think that Vivian had been out back all the time.

When Vivian opened the screen door, the first person she saw was____Mama! Mama was standing at the stove. She wasn't cooking or anything. Just standing there. And sitting around the kitchen table was Jack, Mark, Marlee and Ben. They were all sniffing and wiping their eyes. Crying.

"Mama!" Vivian gasped. "What's wrong, Mama?"

Addie had slowly turned, and with anguished eyes that looked more through, than at Vivian, gestured toward the bedroom. "Your Daddy is gone. He passed away half an hour ago," was her simple statement. "We're waiting for the Undertaker."

If she lived to be one hundred years old, Vivian knew that she would never forget the pain in Mama's eyes. And Vivian also knew that instead of easing that pain, she had probably helped to deepen it.

As she reached Aunt Hettie's house, she pushed open the gate, went through it and around the side of the house to the privacy of the back yard. Slumping down on the back steps, she cried until she was exhausted, never once wiping the mascara that streaked her face.

Grandma Samuels lay on her side watching the flecks of dust dance along the ray of sunshine that formed a bridge, from the opening on the side of the window shade clear down to the floor. With a slow voluntary movement she pushed the light weight blanket off her and sat up. She did not want to waken her oldest granddaughter who was asleep next to her. This was the day of her son-in-law's funeral. A day that she wouldn't mind bypassing altogether. But that was not only impossible, it was unrealistic.

Maybelle slipped her feet into worn slippers and donned the satin dressing gown. A gift from Leon. The last gift that he had given her before he passed away more than two years ago. She was regal in the dark green robe, a tall slender woman whose mature figure enhanced her magnificence. Her long jet-black hair that showed traces of grey at the temples, hung as straight as her deceased Indian mother's. Brown skin and full lips were inherited from her father, and her thin sharp nose sat between high cheeks. The balanced combination resulted in the striking beauty that was sixty year old Maybelle Samuels.

As she tightened the sash of the robe around her waist, she thought of Leon. He had not always been able to give her nice things. Those first years of their marriage had been very hard, with the lack of sufficient money and the way it was for Negroes.

By 1908 Leon decided that it was time to try his luck somewhere else besides Clarksville. Some one had told him that the Southern Pacific railroad was hiring Negro men to work as Pullman porters to "run on the road" between El Paso and Houston.

The only stipulation was that the workers must live in one of the two towns. This was the break he needed, since he wanted to leave northeastern Texas.   Packing his meager belongings, Leon and Maybelle, along with their young daughters, Hettie and Addie, took their first train ride to El Paso. Leon was hired soon after they arrived, and they found a comfortable house on Alamogordo street.

Things began to look up for the Samuels family. One by one, other relatives also moved to the border town, but Maybelle longed for one thing that El Paso could not give her. El Paso was dusty and dry, a fact that they had no way of knowing beforehand. Not that it would have mattered, but deep inside her, Maybelle kept a dream. A dream that one day she would have plants, trees, and flowers growing in abundance. But she didn't spend her time brooding about it, because that was what it was___a dream.

Making her way to the kitchen, she paused as she passed the boys room. Little Andy and Jack shared one bed while Mark and Ben lay, one at the head and the other at the foot of the other bed, tangled up in their covers. Marlee had crawled into bed with Addie the first night after Andy's death, but went back to sleep on a cot the next night in the room with Maybelle and Vivian. Vivian was easy to sleep with because she didn't toss and kick all night the way that Marlee did.

Maybelle set about getting a fire going before Addie and the children woke up. As she poked the smoldering coals in the stove, her thoughts turned to Addie. Poor Addie. Addie must be experiencing this morning some of the very same feelings that she had felt the day of her Leon's funeral. Uncertainty, along with the grief.

Leon had always been blessed with good health, and when he left for work that Monday morning in late May for his run to Houston, he didn't look any different than he usually did, but he did mention having a headache. The train "runs" ordinarily were for four or five days, but two days later he was brought home. He had suffered a stroke, which left him paralyzed. Although the doctor said that he could live many more years, Leon died within a few weeks. He simply lost the will to live. Not long after they first got married he had made an off-handed remark to her, which she had long since forgotten, but obviously he hadn't.

"If I was ever laid up or crippled, and couldn't do for myself....I'd rather be dead than a burden on you." That's what he said, and that was what he meant. The day Maybelle buried Leon she felt as though half of her went into that cold ground with him.

The summer following his death, she had gone, as she always did, to the Baptist National Convention. Her first instinct was to cancel the trip although she and her lady friends had made their plans at last years meeting. She didn't have much of a feel for socializing, but the convention was being held in California. Ever since she was a little girl and heard some of her kin-folks talk about California, she determined to go out there at least once before she died. Sunny, mild, warm California; where orange trees grew in every yard, and a body could see movie stars walking the streets, in person!

Maybelle Samuels fell in love again, but not with a man. Los Angeles, the city of the Angels, stole her heart from the very first. This was the place she had dreamed about without being sure that it really existed. By the end of the convention, she had decided to go back home, pack up and move. And that was what she did.

"Hettie," she declared to her spinster daughter several weeks later; "Since you have your own house over on Myrtle, I'm going to sell this place, because I intend to move to California."

"Mama!" Hettie couldn't believe her ears. "Where in the world did you get such an idea?"

"It's not 'such an idea' at all. I know what I'm doing. All my life I've lived where somebody else wanted me to. First with my mama and daddy, then with your daddy. I never complained, not once. Now, I'm going to live where _I_ want to. It'll be easier for both of us if you don't hinder or try to stop me."

"I know that I can't stop you, Mama, but don't you think that you should think about it for a while?" Hettie argued. "I wouldn't think that one visit to a place would be reason enough to want to move there."

"My mind is made up, Hettie, and that's that!"

Heartsick, but without any more argument, Hettie had helped her mama prepare to move. That had been a time of mixed emotions for Maybelle and both of her daughters. Addie was no more happy about Maybelle's move than Hettie was, but what could she say? Addie had her own family, and the two sisters agreed that Maybelle had a right to her own life now that they were grown and Papa was gone.

"Wouldn't you like to come live with me?" Maybelle had asked Hettie.

"To California? Lord, No." Hettie was vehement. "I don't have any plans to _ever_ leave here. I love El Paso." So Maybelle had moved.

The ticking on the wall clock brought her back to the present. Here she was again, back in El Paso___for another funeral.

Removing one of the lids from the stove, she put several pieces of wood inside. Within minutes the fire was blazing. She rinsed out the coffee pot, measured out fresh water and coffee, and placed the pot on the stove. As she waited for the coffee to perk, she walked to the sink and, pulling back the curtain, gazed out into the back yard. That was when she decided to talk to Addie about moving out to Los Angeles with her. This place would be too much for Addie to manage without Big Andy. In Los Angeles her daughter could have a gas stove instead of this old wooden one. And an electric icebox, too. Not to mention a yard with grass and trees and things. Front and back.

Turning back to the stove she glanced Addie coming down the hall toward the kitchen, her shoulders stooped as though she carried the weight of the world.

Raising her bowed head, Addie greeted her mama in a pitiful voice. "Morning, Mama. I'm sorry you had to make coffee. I meant to get up earlier."

"Don't take any thought to it, Hon. Besides, you need all the rest you can get. Today is going to be real taxing on you. I know." Maybelle beckoned to her daughter, "Come, child. Sit and have some coffee before the children wake up." How she wished that she could spare Addie the days and weeks that lay ahead.

"Addie, hon," she said cautiously. "I'm going to stay on for another week or so to help you get things settled, and I was just thinking...to make it a little easier for you, why don't I take one of the children back home with me? Just for a little while."

"Oh Mama, NO!" Addie's whole body tensed up and her eyes brimmed over with tears. "How could I split up the family? Andy would turn over in his . . . "Her voice trailed off. She couldn't say GRAVE, although they used that phrase all the time. Now it was a reality. Big Andy would soon be in his grave! The thought was almost more than she could bear. Resting one hand on top of the other, she turned her wedding ring round and round on her finger and let the tears flow unchecked.

"It's all right, Hon, " Maybelle said. "Just let it out. I understand. No matter what, remember, that as long as I'm alive, I'll be there when you need me."

Clearly, this was not the time to bring up the subject of moving. After a while Addie wiped her face and sipped from the cup of now lukewarm coffee that Maybelle had sat before her.

"I'm sorry, Mama. I know you meant well___but, no. The children and I___we're gonna stay together. And we'll make it. With the good Lord's help....we will make it."

ALMOST NORMAL

CHAPTER THREE

It's time for me to go home.   That was Maybelle's first thought when she woke up three weeks after Big Andy's funeral. She had twisted and turned all night long, in an attempt to get comfortable. Vivian, who shared the bed, had not appeared to notice, but Maybelle felt that, personally, she couldn't take many more nights in her granddaughters soft bed. She hated to leave Addie and the children, but she had already stayed longer than she had intended to.

Besides the fact that she missed her own bed, she yearned to be in her own house, and with her friends. Not that she didn't have friends here in El Paso, because she did. It was just that she had discovered a whole different world in L.A.. That's what the people out in California called Los Angeles. *I wonder why no one ever called El Paso...E.P.?* She smiled at the thought. *E.P., indeed!*

There was so much to see and do in L.A. that it would, no doubt, take her the rest of her life to see it all, and by then they would probably have added new things. She had gone to the beach; the Hollywood Bowl (which was not really a 'bowl'), the zoo, and parks, parks, and more parks. There was one park, no doubt named after President Abraham Lincoln, which she especially liked.

In Lincoln Park there was a large Merry-go-round, complete with mirrors and sparkling multi-colored stones around the topsides, and in the middle, hidden from view within a hollow round pole, was a pipe organ that played rollicking songs. As the merry-go-round turned round and round, realistic looking carved wooden animals with saddles on their backs, who were mounted on fancy decorated poles, went up and down. Maybelle and one of her lady friends usually spent Sunday afternoons at Lincoln Park, riding the Merry-go-round, eating popcorn, and having a wonderful time.

When they were not at the park they went to a place called an Arboretum, where acres and acres of trees and plants and all sorts of flowers grew.

She had also made friends with three other ladies who were widows, too, and the four of them often went to social functions in the Negro community of L.A.. A few months ago her friends had invited her to join their Thursday afternoon Bridge Club. Maybelle had never so much as had a deck of cards in her house___much less in her hands, but her friends taught her how to play, and she enjoyed it. She had been careful, she was sure, not to mention the subject of playing cards to Addie. Addie had been raised to believe (as was Maybelle) that only "wanton" women played cards.

After dressing, Maybelle went out to the kitchen to lend her daughter a helping hand. That's when she decided that this might be a good time to approach Addie with the idea of moving to L.A. to live with her.

Addie was already cooking breakfast, so Maybelle took on the task of combing and plaiting Marlee's hair. As she sat on her special pillow on the floor in front of her grandma, Marlee grimaced each time that Maybelle pulled the large tooth comb through the young girl's thick hair.

"Grandma! You're hurting me."

"I'm sorry, Baby, but you've just got so much hair." Maybelle replied sympathetically. "Maybe if you tied a scarf on your head at night the way that Vivian does, it wouldn't be so tangled in the morning."

"I tried that, Grandma, but the scarf won't stay on <u>my</u> head."

"Well, Baby, I don't know what else to tell you." *I wouldn't stay on your head if I were a scarf, either,* Maybelle thought. *Not the way you sleep.* To Marlee she said, "It's got to be combed, you know. You don't want to go to school looking like an orphan, now do you?"

"No, ma'am," Marlee sniffed, not really caring how she looked so long as she went. She loved school.

After the children finished eating they collected their books and lunch buckets, which usually contained left-overs from last nights dinner. Kissing their mama and grandma goodby, they hurried out of the house for the long walk to school. Addie stood on the porch, watching them until they were out of sight.

Mark and Marlee were the first ones out of the front gate. They held hands as they strolled down the street, chattering away like two magpies. Andy and Jack followed, occasionally making conversation, but mostly silent, absorbed in their own thoughts.

Vivian brought up the rear. She remained with the group only as far as Joshua Dullums house. Joshua was not ready__as usual, but Vivian sat on the front porch and waited for him__as usual. When he did finally come out of the house, the two of them had to run most of the way to school to keep from being tardy.

When the other children reached Dallas street, they turned south, crossed the Southern Pacific Railroad tracks, and continued down Dallas until they came to Myrtle Avenue. Aunt Hettie lived on Myrtle, and that was where Jack left the little group as he did each day to, "go and see about Aunt Hettie."

When Jack was small Aunt Hettie had told him that he was her favorite nephew. He was not sure exactly why until, at his daddy's funeral, he overheard some of the church sisters talking about Aunt Hettie and Daddy. One of the women said that Aunt Hettie might well have been the grieving widow if Big Andy had fallen in love with her instead of Addie. Aunt Hettie had never mentioned Big Andy in any special way, but Jack suspected that if what the church sister said was true, then his strong resemblance to his Daddy was the reason for the place of favor the he, Jack, occupied. Especially since each morning Aunt Hettie had some special goodie for him to put in his lunch bucket.

Andy and the twins continued east on Myrtle to Eucalyptus Street where they turned south once more, crossed over the Canal, and entered the school yard. Andy was so systematic that he never varied his route, but Jack took a short cut from Aunt Hettie's house and arrived at school about the same time that Andy and the twins did.

Douglas was the only school in El Paso for Negroes, and included grades one through eleven.

Ben remained at home with Addie because he wouldn't be old enough to go to school until the fall. He didn't really mind. Right now he had his mama to himself all day long. When September came, he would be going out of the front gate with the others.

After breakfast, Ben ran out into the backyard to play in the small pond. It wasn't a real pond. Just a hole that Andy and Jack had dug when the weather first turned warm. Addie, who had a great imagination, informed Ben that the two of them would play a game of "let's pretend".

"Let's pretend that the hole is a nice pond, Baby," she said. "And I'll fill the pond with water so's you can play in it. Would you like that?"

"Yes, ma'am. I sure would!"

So each morning Addie carried buckets of water from the kitchen sink out to the pond until it was nearly full. By night time all of the water had soaked into the ground, so the next morning she filled the pond up again. She didn't seem to mind.

"After all," she said, "If it makes my baby happy, then I'm happy, too."

And Ben was happy. And contented. He knew that his mama was close by as he sailed his tiny stick boat back and forth in the pond. When he tired of pushing the little boat he got down in the pond, which was not very deep - only up to his waist - and splashed water, and sang to the top of his lungs. And his mama never fussed at him either, when he tracked mud into the house. Yes, he was a happy little boy.   Inside the house Maybelle washed the breakfast dishes as Addie started the day's dinner. She always tried to do her housework in the back part of the house during the morning hours so that she could keep an eye on Ben. Then in the afternoon, while the boy took a nap, she finished the rest of her chores.

"Addie, Honey," Maybelle said, as she dried the last dish. "Have you given any thought to the future? What you're going to do?"

Addie was kneading dough for her weekly batch of bread. She stopped her task, walked over to the window and looked out to see what Ben was doing.

"I declare, that child loves mud more than a pig," she remarked. Then turning to face her mama she answered, "No, I really haven't, Mama. There are some things that a body would just as soon put off as long as possible."

"Mmm," the older woman mused. "That's probably true. Still, this is something that has to be faced, sooner or later, wouldn't you say?"

Addie nodded her head, then continued kneading the dough.

"This is the way I see it," Maybelle said, reviewing facts that Addie had already struggled with. "The little insurance money that Big Andy left you won't last too long. Maybe through the summer. Then you're going to have to get some kind of work. Probably domestic work since you don't have any training for anything else." Maybelle thought of Addie's short lived college education. "If you manage real close you can make it, money-wise that is, until September. Then if you do get a job what will you do about the children while you are working? Especially Ben? If Andy goes off to college, which it looks like he might, that will leave Vivian in charge. Of course you know that she and that Dullums boy will probably get married next year__if Miss Vivian has her way."

"I know, Mama." Maybelle continued to make her point. "That would throw most of the housework on poor Marlee within the next year, which will be here before you know it. Jack and Mark are good boys, but you can't always count on Jack, especially when he gets moody and disappears to__no telling where. You would always be worrying about them. I hate to sound so pessimistic, but that's the way it is."

"I know," Addie said in a dejected tone, as she rolled out the now pliable dough onto the wooden bread board. Maybelle poured herself a cup of coffee, then went to stand beside her daughter.

"I'd really like for you all to come and live with me in L.A.. I would be there to see to the children while you were at work, to give them hot meals and the correcting that they will most surely need. I've got more than enough room." When Addie made no reply, Maybelle added cheerily, "Besides, Honey, they pay better wages in California than they do here. Who knows, you might get a job working for some movie star, or something."

Addie finished putting the dough into pans, then with resignation she said, "Common sense tells me that I can't make it here alone, but...<u>Oh, Mama</u>," the words seemed to be wrung out of the diminutive widow. <u>"I hate to leave here, and start...all over again!"</u>

"I understand how you feel, Honey. I really do." Maybelle tenderly put her arm around her daughter's shoulder. "It's unfortunate, but we can't always do what we want to in this life. Especially when we have others depending totally on <u>us</u>."

GRADUATION

CHAPTER FOUR

The students marched into the auditorium to the beat of some obscure tune being played on the old upright piano by the music teacher, Mrs. Parker. Andy fastened his eyes on the head of the girl in front of him and tried not to smile as he passed the row of seats where Mama and the rest of his family sat. A sudden tug on his suit coat broke his concentration as Ben leaned into the aisle and shouted, "Andy! Andy!"

"Shush, child," Addie whispered as she took the youngster firmly by the shoulders and set him back in the chair.

Small beads of sweat broke out on Andy's forehead as he took his seat. He was finally graduating with the Douglas High School class of '37! It seemed to him that this day was never going to come, especially after his daddy had died in the early Spring.

Daddy would have been so proud of me, he thought, *what with getting the scholarship. And a full scholarship at that.*

He found it difficult to keep his mind on the monotonous voice of the commencement speaker. *Maybe things are going to work out for me after all. When I finish college I will be able to get a good-paying job and help Mama. Meantime, she will have one less mouth to worry about. It's hard to believe that I'll be gone for four years. but four years isn't a real long time.* He didn't know why he felt guilty. There was no reason to. *It's not my fault that I'm the oldest son. And who started that stupid tradition that the oldest son should take the father's responsibilities when he died?* Andy shifted uneasily in his seat. It was true that he loved his family very much, and he knew as well as the next one that it was going to be pretty tough for Mama without his help. *But I have a right to live my life, too,* he reasoned within himself. *After all, didn't I take over Daddy's job when he got sick? And I still went to school full time. Anyway, when I suggested to Mama that maybe I shouldn't go to college this year__just stay home and work, it was Mama, herself, who said, "No, son. I won't hear of it. You're gonna go to college this year. This is what your daddy and me have planned for a long time. Me and the children are gonna to be just fine." Maybe I'm being selfish, but I worked hard for this.* Andy folded his arms across his chest, comforting himself that he was right.

Addie turned slightly to her right. Pulling her youngest son near, she kissed him affectionately on his black curly head. He looked like a little papoose, so much like his great-grandma.

Ben flashed a wide grin and snuggled as close to his mama as he could. *He's such an adorable child,* she reflected. *It's real easy to love him, and spoil him too.*

To her left sat Vivian. Prissy, Miss Vivian, who had spent the better part of her young life in pursuit of beauty, and Joshua Dullums. Vivian thought that she was in love with Joshua, but what Vivian really was in love with was...Vivian. Addie knew that Vivian was going to give Ben the dickens when they got home for, as she would say "embarrassing me". Vivian hated public displays. Poor Ben. He didn't stand a chance. He was always making "public displays."

"You're spoiling Ben rotten, Mama," Vivian had said several times since Big Andy passed. "You let him get away with things that the rest of us wouldn't even dream of. Daddy would take care of him good fashion...if he were still alive." Her eye's would fill with tears and Ben's unacceptable behavior (another one of Vivian's expressions) was forgotten.

The twins sat between Vivian and thirteen year-old Jack. Next to Jack sat Aunt Hettie. As Addie leaned forward to appraise her brood her heart was wrenched ever so gently by the expression on Jack's face. Three faint creases ran along his high brown forehead that jutted out over deep-set eyes, looking so much like his daddy as he stretched long gangly legs under the chair in front of him. He rarely smiled anymore since Big Andy's death.

Settling back in the rigid wooden chair Addie contemplated once more on Vivian's words, "...if Daddy were alive." *Yes, if Daddy were alive how different things would be, indeed.*

After the funeral, Addie's mama, Maybelle, had convinced her (without much resistance on Addie's part) that the family should move to Los Angeles at the end of summer. Unlike Maybelle, Addie knew that she would never have the same feeling for Maybelle's precious 'L.A.' as she did for this tranquil border town. El Paso was as much a part and partner of her life and happiness as Big Andy had been. Just thinking about it made her heart surge with loneliness for her beloved husband. They had shared so many cherished years together here.

From the beginning of their marriage they had walked around this town together. She taking two steps to each one of his. It was not only because they didn't own an automobile. They just loved to walk. Hand-in-hand they went, from the highest point that they could reach on Mount Franklin, to crossing over the bridge that connected Texas to Juarez, Mexico. They always took the babies - as each one came along - in the perambulator that was Addie's when she was a baby. When each child was big enough to keep up with Big Andy's stride, the next one took his or her place in the pram. They became known as the 'Walking Halls.'

Now all that was changed. The house on Missouri Street had a FOR SALE sign on it, and this would be the last summer (for Lord only knew when) that they would all be together. There was no doubt now that Andy would leave for college in late August, and worst of all, as far as she was concerned, she and the other children would make the long trip to California.

She was thankful that Andy was receiving a scholarship, without which college would be out of the question. Addie determined that no matter how difficult things got, her oldest son was going to go to college. And go this year.

Big Andy didn't have the opportunity to graduate from high school. He hadn't even gone as far as the sixth grade. From the day that Little Andy was born, all his daddy talked about was how he wanted his son to go to college and make something of himself. No one would have ever suspected that Big Andy wasn't educated. Not by the way he talked and conducted himself. He was a fiercely proud man.

As the students rose to receive their diplomas, Addie realized that the commencement program was almost over. It had lasted slightly over an hour. The class was not large. Less than a dozen students, but no small accomplishment for this all Negro school where so many of the young people left before their senior year for one reason or another. Usually economics.

The graduates formed a row of beaming faces as they marched out of the auditorium, down the stairs and into the school yard to accept congratulations from their relatives and friends.

Wrenching free of his mama's grip, Ben ran outside, ahead of the rest of the crowd, to greet Andy, who turned around just in time to catch the small boy up in his arms.

"Andy! Andy!" Ben shrieked. "I saw you standing up there! Did you know I saw you standing up there?" Ben was at the age where he repeated almost everything he said.

"Well, I hoped you would," Andy replied with a grin. "Calm down little guy. Don't talk so loud. You'll fracture my ear-drums," Then leaning away from the boy he asked, "Hey, how did you get away from Mama?"

"Like he always does," retorted Addie, as she and the others approached. "I declare, I don't know what I'm going to do with you, child." Turning her attention to Andy she lovingly patted him on the back. "I'm so proud of you, son." Her eyes glistened with moisture as she pulled his face down to hers and kissed him with all the love a mother could impart.

"I'm proud too, Andy," Ben mimicked. "I'm real proud." "Then get down and let the rest of us congratulate him, will you?" Jack said, extending his hand to his older brother.

Lowering the small boy to the ground Andy grasped Jack's outstretched hand and unexpectedly hugged him, drawing Jack close with his free hand. The two males stood almost eye-to-eye. Both were tall like their daddy. Jack was not sure whether he was as moved by the gesture as he was embarrassed. Andy had never hugged him before, except maybe when he was a baby. It left him with a warm feeling, a feeling of being loved, not requiring anything in return. The way he always felt when, for no reason at all, Daddy used to put his strong manly arm around Jack's shoulder, draw the boy close for a moment and ask, "How be it goin', son?" Those where special times between him and Daddy. How he missed Daddy.

Stepping back to give the others room to congratulate Andy, a dull feeling of despair came over Jack. *Why wasn't it me at Daddy's bedside during those last minutes, instead of Marlee? Just to have spoken to Daddy one last time, to tell him how much I loved him. I wish that I could just sneak off right now, and maybe go walk down the railroad tracks.*

Jack felt a strange attraction to the train tracks, the way that they ran side-by-side, so straight, stretching far, far into the distance. Far, far away, yet going somewhere. Since the death of his daddy he had often walked down the tracks, mile after mile, hurting inside himself, but not being able to cry. Walking until he was almost too exhausted to go back home.

"Jack, are you alright?" Addie had noticed him standing conspicuously apart from the rest of the laughing, teasing group. He did not__no, could not reply as she drew him near to her.

"It's going to get better, son," she whispered with compassion. "Really it is, you'll see. It just takes time."

SWEET TIMES

CHAPTER FIVE

It was that time of evening when the setting sun hadn't quite slipped from view below the horizon - beyond the Rio Grande River, yet the heat of its rays had diminished enough to allow the temperature to be pleasant. An occasional mosquito's presence was felt on a bare arm or leg, but neither heat nor insects were annoying enough to keep the residents of Missouri Street indoors tonight. The air was still and clear, carrying the pleasant sounds of children at play in the humble neighborhood.

There's just no place in this world like El Paso in the late evening, Addie thought. A feeling of peace engulfed her as she sat on the front porch, leisurely rocking back and forth in the old maple rocker that had been her papa's before he died. As she rocked, she decided that, since she couldn't afford to take everything, the chair would be one of the few pieces of furniture that would be shipped to their new home in the west.

Vivian settled on the top step of the porch. Her back rested against the bannister post and her head tilted delicately toward the cloudless western sky. Her dark untroubled eyes revealed nothing of the operation of her mind, which was on Joshua, who, along with her brothers, had gone off to a vacant lot to play touch football. Ben, who always seemed to ask an endless stream of questions when he was around and inactive, had gone next door to play with the two small children who lived over there, so Vivian relished this quiet time without her little brother and happily daydreamed about the love of her young life.

Marlee softly hummed an endless no-name tune as she sat cross-legged near her mama's feet, playing a solitary game of Jacks. The tune was secondary to her concentration on the game. Each time she tossed the small red rubber ball into the air, she tried to scoop up in one hand as many of the jacks as possible, and with the same hand catch the ball on it's downward spiral to the smooth worn surface of the porch floor.

"Marlee," Addie absently cautioned, the rhythm of the rocker matching her words. "You either need to go down on the sidewalk to play, or else quit. You'll be crying if you scoop up a fist full of splinters off this old porch."

The small girl glanced up at her mama momentarily before turning her attention back to the scattered multi-colored jacks. "You say the funniest things, Mama. How can I scoop up a 'fistful of splinters'?" "Keep playing on the porch and you'll find out, Miss." Addie's voice held a tinge of unconcern.

Only the hint of a smile crossed Vivian's otherwise serene face. It seemed like just yesterday that Mama had said the same thing to her. Unlike Marlee, she had not replied, just kept playing. And, she didn't scoop up a fistful of splinters. No, no! She scooped up a plank! At least that's what it felt like. She had learned her lesson the hard way after having the palm of her hand lanced and stitched back up.

As Marlee tossed the ball into the air again, she suddenly paused. With a slight tilt of her head, a quizzical expression replaced the smile on her face as she gazed at her hand in contemplation. The possibility of getting splinters in her hand had really never occurred to her. The red ball, forgotten for the time, plummeted downward unimpeded, bounced on the porch several times, then rolled between two bannister posts and dropped to the ground.

Except for the blinking of her dark eye lids she sat motionless for a long moment. Then, with a resolute gesture she gathered up the jacks, rose to her feet, and with a sheepish grin trotted down the steps, retrieved the red ball, and deposited it along with the jacks into the small cloth bag with the drawstring that Mama had made for her. She mounted the three steps and took a seat opposite Vivian, positioning herself so that she could observe Addie.

"Mama." Marlee's lashes were lowered halfway over her eyes and tiny lines crinkled her chocolate colored brow. In a voice barely above a whisper she asked, "Do you___ miss Daddy?"

Addie continued to rock, her face mobile. Her work worn hands lay crossed in her lap. She seemed engrossed in her thoughts, unaware of her daughter's question.

After what seemed like an eternity passed without any response from Addie, Marlee raised her eyes with trepidation. *Now why would I go and ask something stupid like that? Mama is probably mad at me for asking that.* But Addie was still rocking, expressionless. Marlee sighed with relief. Seemingly Addie had not heard the girl. On the contrary, Addie <u>had</u> heard Marlee. "**<u>You ask if I miss your daddy?</u>**" Addie's reply was vehement, causing Marlee <u>and</u> Vivian to give their mama a startled look. "Only God in heaven knows <u>how much</u> I miss him." Then she lapsed back into silence again, continuing her rhythmic rocking.

Marlee was unsure whether to continue the conversation. The passion with which her mama had replied left the young girl confused. *Mama sounded almost...angry. But at who? Me, or God?* Marlee wondered uneasily. Then shifting her position, she decided to keep her mouth shut and concentrate on the ant that was crawling up the post just above her older sister's neatly curled head. Suddenly the rocking ceased and Addie's mood changed. Her curiosity was aroused. "What made you ask such a question, child?"

The tone of Addie's voice brought back a feeling of relief again to Marlee. With renewed encouragement she jumped up from the steps and went over and stood in front of her mama. She was sure that her mama wasn't angry with _her_. She was _so_ relieved that she launched into a detailed answer with all the drama of a ten-year old.

Putting her hands on her hips the way she had seen the older women do when they were having an "I said" and "she said" conversation, she declared, all in one breath, "Well, you know my best friend Benita? Well, she said that her mama cried for almost a year after her daddy died, and I said that you hadn't cried since Daddy's funeral, and she said that her mama said that if a body didn't cry much, that they must not miss the one who died too much, and I said..."

"Marlee!" Vivian gave the hem of Marlee's dress a sharp jerk, causing the smaller girl to nearly lose her balance. "Don't keep going on and on. Get to the point, will you?"

"**I'm** not talking to **you!**" Marlee snapped at Vivian. "I'm talking to Mama. And quit pulling on my dress."   Turning   her attention back to her mama, Marlee continued, "And so I said..." She was just starting to wind up again when Addie interrupted her.

"_Mar--lee_! So what you want to know is___if I'm grieving, then why don't I cry for a year? Is that right?" Addie wasn't sure whether she was more irritated at Marlee, or Benita's mama. *A year of crying, indeed. I know Benita's mama quite well, and that lady was crying long before her husband had thought of dying. Crying was her way of keeping him under control. Maybe he died because he got tired of her eternal sniveling.* Keeping her thoughts to herself she answered Marlee in a way that she hoped would satisfy her talkative daughter, who would more than likely repeat the conversation to Benita.

"You see baby," she measured her words, "some folk cry on the outside, and some folk cry on the inside." She paused to let her words sink in. "I guess I'm just one of those <u>inside</u> folk."

"Oh!" Marlee replied. *Of course,* she thought. *Why didn't <u>I think of that?</u>*

"Mama," Vivian said exasperated, "let's change the subject. All this talk about crying and whatnot is beginning to depress me. Tell me, what do you think about Los Angeles? I mean, what do you think that it's really like?"

"Personally, I don't know, but your grandma has nothing but 'high praise' for the place." Addie was glad to change the subject, too.

"Do you believe that movie stars walk the streets like everyday people?" Vivian persisted.

"I think Grandma was pulling our leg, God love her soul." Addie smiled at the question. "She'd probably tell us anything to convince us that Los Angeles was the best thing that happened since sweet butter."

Vivian and Marlee looked at each other, then giggled knowingly. Addie was beginning to sound like her old self again.

"And I'll tell you something else." Addie leaned back in the rocker with a smug "have I got a secret" look on her face. "Your grandma plays cards."

"Cards!" Echoed the girls in astonishment. "Yes, cards. They call it Bridge, but it's just cards to me. She let it slip one day when she was telling me all about the 'glorious city.' I pretended as though I didn't catch it, but I did. She thinks I don't know about anything but keeping house and having babies." Addie paused, then added with amusement, "Can you imagine Grandma playing cards?"

The vision of Maybelle sitting at a table with playing cards spread fan-style in her hand, trying to look like she knew what she was doing, not only struck Addie as funny, it was hilarious. Slapping her leg, she threw her head back and laughed, a deep delicious, rippling sound. The two girls doubled over with glee.

Marlee, always the bold one, proceeded to go a step further. She launched into an imitation of a shaky old woman with a deck of imaginary cards, tilting her head to the side, she held her hand, first up close, then out at a distance from her, squinting and trying to focus on the cards, all the while shaking. Her impression made Addie and Vivian laugh even harder, until Addie remembered that__*this is my ten-year old carrying on like she was grown!*

With no small amount of difficulty she managed a straight face and said, "All right Marlee. That's enough of that. You should be ashamed of yourself, making fun of your grandma. And I'm ashamed for starting it."

Deep down inside she had to admit one thing. That little devilish daughter of hers was the funniest thing she had seen for a long time. Too long. The laughter was like a healing balm, causing the vise that gripped her heart to begin to loosen a trifle.

School had been out less than a month, but Jack and Mark were already running out of something to do after all their chores were done. Of course there was the usual football, marbles, and riding the scooter that they finally finished after Big Andy's funeral. However, the wheels of the scooter kept falling off. First one, and then the other, so, after a few days, they grew tired of repairing it and dumped the homemade scooter in the back yard along with the rest of the old wagon.

Andy had very little time to play with the two boys anymore. After his graduation the railroad had hired him as a permanent 'redcap' porter. When he wasn't at work or doing chores for Mama, he took Big Andy's bicycle and peddled out to east El Paso to visit with a classmate named Sarah Perkins. He claimed that he wasn't courting Sarah. That they were just good friends. Addie hoped that Sarah knew that was what she and Andy were. Just good friends!

The days gradually got hotter. The kind of heat that hangs out there like a blanket that kind of covers you in the middle of the day, dragging the strength out of you and up into the clear blue sky where one can see straight to eternity. On these days, the wise thing to do is to get up early, do chores, and spend the early afternoon taking a nap, if possible. People in this part of the country call it "taking a siesta". Between late afternoon and early evening, the weather begins to cool off, and everybody comes out of doors___folks and things.

Up and down the streets, all over town, folk could be seen sitting on covered porches in rocking chairs and swings, and tiny babies lay in buggies or on pallets in a protected corner of the porch. The smaller children played in the fenced-in yards; running, jumping and laughing gleefully as they enjoyed the outdoors. Most of the teenage boys and girls looked forward to the late evening when they could go for long walks with their friends, out of sight of the adults.

This particular evening, Addie, along with Marlee and Ben, walked over to Myrtle Avenue to visit with Aunt Hettie. Vivian and Joshua, along with Andy and Sarah, decided to walk across the bridge to do some 'eye-buying' in Juarez. That left Jack and Mark to their own devices, with a warning from Mama to behave themselves and stay out of mischief.

Several years earlier Big Andy had bought Marlee a large doll that walked when it was wound up with a key in it's back, along with a buggy for the doll. At first Marlee would not let anyone touch the doll or buggy, and kept them close by her bed when she wasn't pushing the buggy around the yard, singing to the doll and sometimes scolding it. But, for the last year, since marbles and jacks came into her life, the doll and buggy sat unnoticed in the bedroom that she and Vivian shared.

As Jack and Mark loafed on the porch pondering what to do with their time, one of them came up with the idea of using Marlee's buggy for a ride down Octavia Street. Octavia was steep enough for them to get a swift, exhilarating ride downhill before the street leveled out one block before it reached Missouri Street.

They agreed that it would be better if Marlee didn't know anything about their little adventure, so they planned to get the buggy back in its place before she and Mama returned home.

Hurrying inside, they took the doll from the buggy and laid it on the bed, along with the tiny quilt and lace pillow that Mama had made. Jack pushed the buggy - with Mark close behind - out of the house and through the gate (not forgetting to latch it), trying to ignore the questioning expressions of neighbors as they strolled nonchalantly down their street westward until they reached Octavia. Once they turned the corner, they quickened their pace as they started the uphill ascent.

The first cross street was Wyoming. From there on the incline grew sharper, so the boys decided to trot so as to reach their destination as soon as possible. At this point they ceased to be concerned about anyone seeing them pushing a doll buggy (something that they weren't too proud of), because all of the houses from Wyoming Street northward belonged to well-to-do white people who sat out in the back of their houses on screened porches. There was little or no activity out front, except possibly a gardener.

The two boys jogged steadily up the street for more than three very long blocks. At least they seemed very long to ten year old Mark.

"Let's stop here," he panted. "I'm almost out of breath." Without waiting for an answer he released the buggy handle and collapsed on the curb. Jack took a few more steps, and he too dropped to the grass that grew between the sidewalk and the street, turning the buggy on its side to keep it from rolling backward downhill.

They both lay on the grass, taking gulps of the cool evening air. Finally Jack got to his feet and said, "Come on, Mark. Let's get started. It will be dark before too long. Since this was my idea, and I'm the oldest, I'll ride first, alright?"

Mark readily conceded, because with the excitement of the anticipated buggy ride, he had forgotten one important detail. He was forbidden out of the yard without permission! Jack had no problem, provided that they didn't get caught with the buggy, since he was almost fourteen and didn't need consent. The thought had come to Mark as he rested on the curb. He just wanted to get back home before Mama did. Taking Marlee's buggy was nothing compared to disobeying. No doubt about it, he would surely get a good whipping from Mama.

Meanwhile, Jack had sat the doll buggy in the middle of the street and was beckoning to Mark to hold it firmly so that Jack, who was much too tall to sit in the little buggy, could straddle it.

"Give me a good push, and when I get going you follow behind me." Jack instructed his brother. "I'll stop before we get to our street. Then I'll help you push the buggy back up and you can ride. I'll follow you down in case you have trouble stopping. By then, if we want to, we can go on home, alright?"

Whenever Jack told Mark anything he always ended it with "alright?", or "you got it?". This time Mark wanted to say, "NO, it's not alright," because he wanted to go home. Now! Instead he replied, "Alright. I got it," because he just wanted to get going.

Mark gave the buggy a running push and Jack took off down the street, his long gangly legs dangled on each side of the little buggy as it sailed along. Gaining momentum, it passed the first block, then the second. Mark followed close behind, his feet moving so fast that they seemed not to touch the pavement.

Running downhill is almost as much fun as riding, Mark thought as they laughed gleefully. For a brief time everything else was forgotten. *This is really great*!

As the buggy bearing the tall boy approached Wyoming - the beginning of flat ground - an automobile turned the corner, heading slowly up Octavia. It didn't seem to present any immediate danger to the boys because, first of all the automobile was not moving more than ten miles an hour, and more important, Jack saw the automobile. But__alas, Mark didn't! Jamming his feet into the pavement to act as brakes, Jack brought the buggy to a sudden stop, and poor Mark ran headlong into him, propelling both of them onto the street. Jack went one way, Mark went another, and Marlee's doll buggy sailed end over end through the air and landed in the direct path of one of the front wheels of the huge Hupmobile automobile!

The white gentleman who was driving jammed on the brakes, stopping the automobile, but seconds too late to save the buggy. Jumping out, he ran over to the two boys to see if anyone was hurt. They were not. Just scared silly! The considerate man backed up his automobile, got out again and removed what was left of the buggy, handed it to Jack, asked the boys for their address (offering to replace the mangled toy), got back into his automobile, and drove on up the street.

Mark was completely dazed and began to cry. He didn't even know what had hit him. He calmed down a little, after Jack assured him that it wasn't the automobile. Just Jack's back! Then he remembered his other woe. Mama was not only going to whip him____she was going to kill him! Not to speak of his quick tempered sister.

That night, as well as the next couple of weeks, would go down in infamy for Jack and Mark Hall. They had pulled some stunts in their time, but this topped it. Everything would have been fine if there hadn't been all those "if'n's". If Jack had started down the street a few seconds earlier; If Mark hadn't been running so close behind him; If the large Hupmobile had not turned the corner when it did; If Mama hadn't decided to return home earlier than expected, and If the doll buggy were still a doll buggy instead of a heap of scrap___then what followed when they reached home would, no doubt, never have happened.

When the two bedraggled boys reached the front gate the first thing that they heard was Marlee, inside the house having a hissy-fit. She had discovered the abduction of her precious doll-baby's buggy. It was at that point that Mark suggested that they go across the river to Mexico for a while___until things cooled down.

While they were in the decisive stage who should come up but...Andy and Vivian! And Jack was still holding the evidence. Between Marlee's mouth - which could be heard for miles around, it seemed - and the mangled buggy, it didn't take Andy very long to figure out what had happened. The situation could only progress one way. Worse!

Andy marched the two boys into the house, his strong hands gripping the back of their necks. Marlee had to be physically restrained following Jack's remark that she, "didn't have to foam at the mouth, since the kind gentleman said that he was going to buy her another, probably better, buggy." He almost found out how strong she really was, along with her temper.

Mama made them relate the whole story, down to the smallest detail. She was calm up until they came to the part about the Hupmobile. That's when she lost it.

"You could have been hurt. Or worse__, killed! What in this world were you thinking about? Is your head filled with air? Isn't it bad enough that we're trying to get over one death in this family? Don't I have enough to worry about? And if that wasn't bad enough, you took something that wasn't yours?"

On and on she went. Jack wished she would just go ahead and whip them and get it over with.

Up until now Mark had stood slightly behind Jack and kept silent, but in an unwise attempt to convince Addie that they were never in any real danger, he spoke up.

"But Mama. The automobile didn't hit us. I ran into Jack and knocked him off of the buggy."

Addie reached around Jack, grabbed Mark by the front of his shirt and pulled the boy from the safety of his older brother before Mark knew what was happening. Her eyes withered him, and the threatening sound of her voice convinced him that he and Jack should have gone to Mexico. "So, young man. You caused the accident, did you? Well, thanks for reminding me. If you had obeyed and stayed in the yard where you belonged, you wouldn't be about to get your hide tanned as soon as I finish with Mister Jackson."

Jackson! Jackson! Jack was shocked. Neither Mama nor Daddy had ever called him Jackson before. Everyone knew how much he hated that name. Jack viewed this as his mama's act of disowning him. As if she didn't love him anymore!

Addie could not have anticipated what happened next, nor could anyone else, including Jack. Without warning, he fell on his knees, his body trembling violently as it was racked with terrible heart-wrenching sobs. Grief over his beloved daddy's death, too long pent up inside him, was finally released.

"I'm sorry, Mama. I'm really, really sorry. I'm sorry that I disappointed you. Mama, oh Mama. I'm sorry." Over and over he wailed. Then, "Daddy, Daddy___I'm sorry Daddy." It seemed as though his very heart would shatter because of the intense pain he felt.

In an instant Addie was beside her son, and lifting him to his feet, she led him to the settee. She cradled his head to her bosom, and rocking him like a lonely baby, she let him cry it all out. All the heartache and sorrow that he had not been able to express since losing his dearest friend. His daddy.

Vivian and Andy took the other children out back. This was one of those times that was too intimate for the rest of them to share.

Marlee was touched with compassion for her brother that night, but the next day was another story. Somebody had to pay for the loss of her precious buggy, and she wasn't talking about the man in the automobile, either. She didn't have the heart to say any more to Jack after last night. So, that left only one other person.

For the first time, and the last, he hoped, Mark fell out of favor with his beloved twin. For two agonizing weeks she punished him with a fate worse than death - literally. She refused to say one single word to him, or even acknowledge his presence. And...he still got a whipping from Mama!

After the "borrowed buggy" incident things had been quiet on Missouri Street. The commotion at the Hall house had not gone unnoticed in the neighborhood. Mother's jumped on it as an opportunity to impress a point upon their young ones.

"Now do you see what happens when you disobey? Remember," they knowingly added, "what's done in the dark, will soon come to light."

The children weren't sure that "dark" meant that Jack and Mark did what they did in the night___or that they did it in___secret. Either way, the results were less than desirable.

The 'Hupmobile' gentleman was true to his word. He sent a beautiful doll carriage - not just a plain old buggy - to Marlee. It must have cost twice as much as the one Daddy had bought, but Marlee didn't care. She was still angry with the boys.

"This is a real nice doll carriage, don't you think, baby," Addie remarked of the buggy. "I hope you're not still holding a grudge against your brothers. If I can forgive them, surely you can."

"I guess so, Mama," she replied in a sullen tone. The way Mama put it, what else could she say. Her so-called punishment of Mark turned out to be as painful (if not more so) to her as it was to him. Not talking to Mark was worse than not talking to herself, which was like not talking at all. And not being able to talk, as far as she was concerned, was the same as being dead. If that wasn't bad enough, Mark had shown himself to be as thoughtless as Jack. *Mark knew more than any body else in the whole world how much that buggy meant to me*, Marlee sulked, *because Daddy gave it to me. Now it's gone____and so is Daddy.*

"I'll forgive them, but it will be a long, long time before I forget." She folded her arms tightly across her chest, clamped her quivering lips together to keep from Crying, and stared at the floor.

"Mama___Mama!" Ben called from the back yard.

"I wonder what that child wants now?" Addie demanded, wiping her hands on her apron. She had been trying all morning to get the breakfast dishes finished. Marlee sat at the kitchen table humming her usual no-name song as she shelled peas for dinner. The other boys had gone to work with Andy, and Vivian was earning extra money helping Aunt Hettie.

Ben was usually pretty good about playing alone, but not today. "Mama___Mama!" He called again.

"I'm coming, Ben," Addie called back. "Just hold your horses." And to Marlee, "Get the comb so's I can do something with your hair. I'll be right back."

Marlee shook her head in disgust. You would think that Ben was a king or something. Every time he calls, Mama goes to see what he wants.

"I don't need my hair combed," she muttered defiantly. "I'm not going anywhere." She may have gotten the back of Mama's hand across her mouth for being sassy, but Addie didn't hear her. Addie had gone outside to see what her baby wanted.

"What is it, Ben?"

"Can I please go next door to play with Teddy?" He pleaded.

"No, you certainly cannot. You were just over there yesterday. You know what I told you about wearing out your welcome, don't you?"

"Yes, ma'am," he replied with sorrowful eyes. "But I don't have anybody to play with."

Addie sat down on the step and drew Ben onto her lap. "I know, baby. Mama and Marlee have too much to do to play with you right now. Why don't you get your ball and play with it, and maybe, after supper, we'll all walk down town to the movie house. Would you like that?"

Ben brightened up at once. "Yea! Yea!" he threw his arms around Addie's neck and squeezed her tight. Kissing him, she put him down and rose to go back inside.

At the door she admonished him firmly, "Ben, don't go out of the yard. Do you understand me?"

Ben understood. "Yes, ma'am. I won't." Mark's whipping was still fresh in Ben's young mind. He nodded his head as he headed for the front yard, and his ball.

Marlee sat on the floor on her special pillow, in front of Mama's chair, the comb in her hand and a frown on her face. There has got to be some way to make this hair-combing feel better, she thought. *Maybe I could get Mama to cut my hair short like the boys. No, that wouldn't work. All the kids in the neighborhood would laugh and make fun of me. There must be something. My scalp can't take it much longer. Why was I born tender-headed? Why couldn't my hair have been like Ben's? Or even Benita's? Of course Benita wasn't born with straight hair, but she said that her mama got tired of struggling with Benita's kinky hair years ago, so she...That's the answer! Straighten! Why didn't I think of that before?*

She could hardly wait for her mama to come back in the house. "Mama," she said happily. Addie had returned and began to un-braid the thick plaits. "I've got the answer!" "Answer to what, child? I didn't ask you anything." "To my hair. So it won't hurt so much when you comb it."

"And what is the answer? You know that your hair has got to be combed. Marlee. We go through this every day."

Marlee scrambled up, turned, knelt down on the pillow and rested her elbows in Addie's lap. Her almond shaped eyes were serious as she gazed directly into Addie's face.

"You can straighten it!" she announced triumphantly. "Marlee Hall! Where did you get such an idea? You know what I think about putting a hot comb on little girl's hair."

"But Mama___not a <u>hot,</u> hot-comb. Just a warm hot-comb. Benita said that's what her mama does to her hair, and she is the same age I am. Straightens her hair with a warm hot-comb."

I should've known it, Addie thought. *Some more of this 'Benita said' stuff. Still, it's not a bad idea. She felt sorry for Marlee every time the girl's thick mop of hair had to be combed. Of course, It would never do to let this child think that I would even think of taking the advice of a ten year old. She's womanish enough as it is.*

"Your grandma suggested that when she was here. Straightening your hair. Truthfully speaking, I forgot all about it, what with your daddy passing away and all. I'll give it some serious thought, though." Maybelle had mentioned something about Marlee's thick hair, but the suggestion had gone in one ear, and out of the other. "Turn around now child, so's I can get through or I'll never get my other work done."

She barely got the words out of her mouth when they heard Ben screaming again. "Mama! Mama!" This time he sounded urgent.

Addie moved the girl aside and stood up. On her way to the door she remarked with exasperation, "I declare, that boy is gonna to drive me crazy. I'm just gonna to have to bring him in and put him down for a nap."

Marlee was more than glad for an interruption. Anything to get Mama off of her head. She followed Addie outside as Ben continued to call, "Mama." By now the screams had resolved into whimpering. The sight that greeted Addie almost caused her to burst into laughter.

There was Ben, on his hands and knees - at least on one hand - with his head and part of his body wedged between the pickets of the next door neighbor's fence! On the other side, a hands length out of reach, lay his ball.

Ben looked so funny. All he had to do was scoot back into the their yard and he would be free, but instead, he kept crying and pushing forward, twisting and turning. Kneeling beside the crying, squirming boy Addie said, "Hush Ben. You're not dying." She tried to sound stern, but she felt like joining Marlee who was howling with glee, enjoying the whole scene. *Serves him right*, Addie thought. *He is forever getting into something*. She gently bent his shoulder forward toward his chest, turning him sideways, and pulled him back from between the pickets.

"What possessed you to stick your big head between those pickets?" She asked, wiping his dirty, tear-stained face with her apron. "Didn't you know you'd get stuck?"

"No, ma'am," he sniffed. "I didn't think about it. I just wanted my ball___and you said___'don't go out of the yard, Ben'."

ADIOS AND SO LONG

CHAPTER SIX

Grandma Samuels once said, "You don't know how much stuff you have until you decide to move." Grandma was so right.

It was the second week in August, summer was almost over, and the house had been sold to a family stationed out at Fort Bliss who wanted to move in by the first of September. Since Andy was scheduled to be in Austin for enrollment in college on the twenty-eighth of August, Addie planned that they would all leave on the same day. Andy would be taking the train going southeast, and she and the other children would board the westbound train to L.A., as Grandma Samuels fondly called Los Angeles.

There was still a lot to do. Different of the neighbors bought most of the furniture. Some of it had already been taken away, and the rest; like the beds, the kitchen table, and the chairs, the settee, and the ice box were to be picked up after the family left. Aunt Hettie had agreed to keep Addie's treasured upright piano until the family got settled and Addie could send for it. The wood-burning stove would be left in the house.

Jack and Mark brought cardboard boxes from the grocery store for Addie and the girls to pack the family's personal belongings in, and Andy's boss was nice enough to loan him an antiquated flat-bed truck for hauling away heavy things.

The only furniture that would be shipped to California was the Singer sewing machine, Papa Samuels's rocking chair, and the Steamer trunk that had sat, mysterious and closed, in one corner of Big Andy and Addie's bedroom for as long as any of the children could remember.

When they first started packing, Vivian suggested that they tackle one room at a time. Addie agreed. In this way there would be less chance of the girls getting rid of something that was precious to her.

Today they were working in Addie's bedroom. "Mama, what about this trunk?" Vivian inquired as she rattled the lock of the Steamer trunk. "Do you have a key? I can't get it open." "I'm sure I do___somewhere." Addie continued packing a box of clothes. "Don't you want me to open it?" "I guess so," Addie answered hesitantly. Still she folded and stowed garments into the box in front of her.

Vivian frowned with impatience as she stood with one hand on the trunk lock, and the other hand on her hip. *Mama acts like she doesn't want to open the trunk. What could be in there that's such a secret?* She wondered.

"Mama?" Vivian inquired again, but Addie merely set her mouth and continued her task. When the box was full she closed the top, tied it securely with hemp-string, and pushed it over in one corner of the room next to the other boxes. Going over to her bed, she lifted the foot of the mattress and retrieved a small brocade coin purse from a paper sack that lay between the mattress and the springs. She unsnapped the purse and took out a key.

Addressing the two girls, she spoke somberly, "No doubt you all have wondered why we kept this trunk locked. Well, darlings, I think it's time for you to see. What's inside is very important and precious to me...and was to your daddy."

Tears rose to the surface of her eyes. Her husband's death in the early spring still left the pall of grief lingering in her heart and the house. She drew on some deep inner strength, and continued. "I'm hoping that you girls will feel the same way. You see, this trunk and what is inside is all that Big Andy and I have to leave to you children. This is what you might call___your inheritance. Do you understand?"

"I think so, Mama," Vivian replied, not actually sure that she did. Marlee nodded. She understood even less, but she liked being in on grown folks things, so she mirrored Vivian's knowing look and kept her mouth shut.

The Steamer trunk was about thirty-six inches high and two feet deep. It was made of a dark colored sheet metal and stood on it's side instead of laying on it's bottom. Addie inserted the key into a large round brass lock, which popped open. She unfastened two latches, above and below the lock, and swung the lock back. Scooting the trunk away from the wall, she opened it by pushing outward on both sides. Something like splitting open a peach. The two girls stared in wonderment. They had never seen the trunk open before.

The Steamer trunk was fascinating on the inside. It was lined with a pale flowered kind of heavy paper, like wall paper. One side was like a chest of drawers. Small drawers at the top, and larger ones below. The other side was like a closet, with a round wooden pole near the top that stretched from front to back, with fancy shaped coat hangers hanging on it. Each hanger held an article of clothing. The odor of mothballs floated into the bedroom from some unseen place within the trunk. There were two men's coats; one looked fashionable, and the other one was old and worn. A long white lacy dress, a beautiful multi-color blanket, a cap that was pinned to the hanger, a baby quilt, and a white smock-type coat.

Vivian and Marlee gave each other questioning glances. *Just some old clothes. What's so precious about old clothes*, they wondered.   "Sit down, and listen good," Addie said motioning them to the bed. "I can imagine what you're thinking, that these are just a lot of old things. Well, you're thinking wrong."

Taking the first coat from it's hanger she explained solemnly, "This belonged to your daddy's papa. His name was Jackson. Jackson Emery Hall. He was born sometime around 1870 in Milledgeville, Georgia. Big Andy wasn't sure. That's what they told him. Your daddy was near ten years old when Jackson died. A run-away horse-drawn buggy turned over on him. This coat was the only thing that your daddy had left...to remember his papa by."

As Addie hung the coat back in the trunk Marlee felt something draining from her. She realized that she had secretly been angry with her daddy for dying, leaving her when she was so young and the two of them had really gotten to know each other. But seeing that old worn coat, and hearing how her daddy had also lost his papa released every bit of anger, because she had so very much more to remember Big Andy by. She had her mama, and Viv, and her brothers. Not to mention Grandma and aunt Hettie.

Addie touched the next coat. She did not take it out, just ran her hand along the sleeve several times. "This is the coat that your daddy wore when we got married." That was all she said.

Removing the next article she said, "This blanket was made by your great-grandma. Grandma Samuels's mama. She was called Delia, but her Indian name was Pleasant Face. She was born in Oklahoma on the fifteenth of September, in 1860." Addie smiled, pleased that she knew, and remembered her grandma's birthday. "My grandma wove this blanket herself and gave it to her husband Benjamin, as a wedding present. They had sixteen children, your

Grandma Samuels being the youngest."   "Did you name Ben after great-grandpa?" Marlee asked.

"Yes, we certainly did," Addie replied as she returned the blanket to the hanger. "Ben inherited great-grandpa's name, and Vivian inherited great-grandma Delia's hair."
Vivian beamed and stroked her hair.

Wonderful! Marlee thought ruefully. *And just what did I inherit? My hair is thick___but kinky, my legs are long and skinny, and I am the darkest one in the family.* Before she had a chance to work herself into a fit of self-pity Addie removed the delicate white dress from the hanger.

"This, young ladies, is my wedding dress."   Addie's face became radiant as she displayed the garment. "Isn't it beautiful?"

It was more than just beautiful. It was breathtaking. Soft water-marked taffeta covered with delicate airy lace formed the full floor-length dress. A wide satin ribbon, that could be tied into a large bow, was tacked at the small waist. The bodice front was pleated, and in the back of the dress tiny satin covered buttons ran from a few inches below the waist up to the high collar. Miniature silk roses bordered the neck and cuffs of the sleeves, and rows of seed-pearls had been painstakingly sewn down the front of the gown, from the high neck, to the hem.

"Oh, Mama!" Vivian proclaimed. "It's so...!" "I know,"
Addie glowed as though this was her very first time seeing the gown.

Vivian jumped up, took the gown out of her mama's hands, and being thoroughly delighted, began waltzing around the room, singing as she held the dress up in front of her. Marlee clapped approval as she sang along with her sister.   "Be   careful   now, child," Addie cautioned. "My mama spent a lot of time making that dress, and I promised her that I would pass it down to my daughters one day." She had a faraway look as she thought of the day she wore the dress. Then turning back to the trunk, she said, "Let me finish, now. You can try on the dress later, if you're real careful."

Vivian hugged the dress to her and sat back on the bed beside Marlee, who had not the least interest in wedding gowns, or marriage.

"Go on, Mama," Vivian coaxed. "Tell us about the baby quilt."

"In due time," Addie replied. "First, let me tell you about this cap. This was your daddy's. This was the cap that the railroad gave him when he first started as a 'Redcap," and didn't have to be a roustabout any more. That was a big step up for him. He came in contact with a lot of high class people over the years. He always liked the finer things of life even if he didn't have an education."

"Can I hold it, Mama?" Marlee was fascinated with the cap. It was bright red, with a black shiny bib. "Can I put it on my head, please?"

Addie's first response was, "No." Then she changed her mind. "Alright, child. Go on. Put it on. Maybe some of your daddy's patience and calm spirit will rub off on you."

Marlee took her mama's remark as a compliment. *Oh, to be like Daddy, who had been so loving and kind.* She plopped the cap on her head. Already she felt different. Kind of warm and comforted, like Daddy was near.

The white smock-like coat was next. "This was my papa's pullman porter coat. He was wearing it the day they brought him home, with a stroke, before he died." There wasn't any need to say more. They all knew the rest.

The only thing left was the baby quilt. Addie held it in her arms, close to her heart, for a long time. Something about the quilt, and the way that her mama held it stirred vague pictures in Vivian's mind. She couldn't quite put it together. She had been so small when it happened. "Mama, whose quilt was that?" she gently asked. "Lawrence's," Addie said with a far-a-way look in her eyes. "Your baby brother." Marlee gasped! *Baby brother?* She thought, too surprised to say a word.

That was it! Vivian thought. *A baby. A baby who went away and never came back. No one talked about the baby after he left. Mama had cried a lot, and then later, much later, there was another baby. Jack. Mama didn't cry anymore after Jack came.*

Addie continued before either of the girls could speak. "Lawrence was born after you, Vivian. He was a big healthy baby. I nursed all of you children until you were over a year old, you know. Well, one day when Lawrence was ten months old...I had a taste for cabbage." She paused, fighting back hot tears as she re-lived that painful time. "I wasn't thinking, I guess. Cabbage is terrible for a nursing mother. It causes gas, and the gas is passed through the milk to the baby." She paused again, put her hand to her mouth and sighed, "Mmm." Looking into Vivian's eyes she continued sadly, "Poor little Lawrence, he just couldn't pass the gas. He had colic. The doctor couldn't figure out what was causing him to be so sick for two whole weeks. I had forgotten all about the cabbage. Then, when Dr. Rivers did__ figure out what was wrong___ my baby had cried and suffered so that his little heart was just wore out. Crying and hurting all that time. I was so broke...up..." Addie struggled to talk, steadily rocking the empty baby quilt. "I didn't think I could live. The grief was bad. But you know, it was the guilt. The guilt almost took me away." She drew in a deep breath. "Dr. Rivers said that we needed to have another baby right away. I didn't want to, but your daddy thought we should. So we did. But we never spoke of Lawrence again." She took a handkerchief from the pocket of her apron, removed her eyeglasses, and wiped away the tears that trickled down her face. "This is the first time I've been able to speak my baby's name in fourteen years, but I wanted you girls to know about him. I'll tell the boys later." Addie put the tiny blue and white quilt back onto it's hanger. She closed the trunk. "I'll tell you what's in the drawers another day. I'm plumb drained out, right now, and I still have more packing to do."

The two girls remained sitting on the bed as Addie left the room. Marlee, with Daddy's cap on her head, and Vivian clutching Mama's wedding dress to her bosom. They were plumb drained out, too.

Less than one week remained before they would board the train. Addie tucked the train tickets into the pocketbook that she would carry on the trip. Most of the cash money she would pin inside of her slip, except what she would need on the train, and___that portion that was for Andy.

Marlee sat on her special pillow as Addie tied a ribbon on the last plait of the girl's head. Addie had finally broken down and straightened the little girl's hair. She was amazed how long Marlee's hair really was. At least two inches longer, hanging to the child's elbow. Addie wished she had straightened the thick kinky hair much earlier. These daily times would have been much more pleasant for both of them.

"Baby, do you want to go out to Benita's house to say goodby?" Addie asked.

"Could I, Mama? Would you take me out there?" Marlee's face lit up. Benita lived in east El Paso not far from Aunt Hettie's house. They were in the same grade, but visits with her very best friend in the summer time were few and far between. She had not let herself think about what school in California would be like without Benita. She had not let herself think about California at all. She was like mama. *How could anyone - except Grandma Samuels, and maybe Vivian - want to leave El Paso?* she wondered.

"We'll go out there tomorrow, early. You, Me and Ben. You can spend the better part of the day at Benita's. Ben and I will pay Hettie a last visit. I'll send Andy to tell Benita's mama that you'll be coming." Addie gave Marlee a hug, then went to the kitchen to start dinner.

After breakfast the next morning Addie, along with the two children, headed down Missouri Street eastward for their farewell visit with Hettie and Benita. Jack and Mark went to the railroad station with Andy. Andy's boss had hired them these last two weeks to work around the depot so that they could earn some extra money for the trip. Vivian would be leaving the house later to meet Joshua. They planned to go up to Las Cruses with Joshua's uncle who had an automobile. Vivian assured her mama that they would be back before midnight.

Benita was sitting on her front steps, patiently waiting to see her dearest friend for what___her mama said___ might be the last time, when she saw Marlee coming. "Marlee!" Benita shouted, as Marlee came closer. Benita bolted out of the gate, leaving it open.

"Benita!" Marlee turned Mama's hand loose and dashed toward her friend. The two girls met halfway. They hugged each other, then took hands and skipped back to Benita's yard, giggling and chattering, and stopping every few steps to hug each other.

Addie and Ben followed the little girls, stopping just outside the gate.

"Benita," Addie called out, "Tell your mama that I'll stop in on my way back and visit with her. Marlee, you behave yourself now, you hear me?"

"I will, Mama." Marlee called back, as she and Benita were on their way to the back yard to enjoy their time together. Benita's yard had a giant old tree in it, with a swing hanging from one of the branches. The girls took turns. One sat in the swing while the other one pushed. Back and forth, higher and higher, spindly legs stretched out until their feet seemed to touch the blue sky. When they tired of the swing, Benita brought out her rag dolls, and a tiny tea set. Her mama made a pitcher of lemonade, and peanut butter and jelly sandwiches for their lunch. By now the sun was straight over head, so they decided to rest under the tree on an old blanket. To rest and talk.

"Will you promise to write to me, Benita?" Marlee asked. "Every day. Well, maybe not every, every day, but real regular. And will you write to me, too?" The two thin girls lay on their backs with their feet against the tree trunk, hands locked behind their heads.

"Of course I will, since it was my idea. We'll always be friends, and you know what... when I get grown, I'm going to move back here and we can live next door to each other."

"Really, Marlee?" Benita asked. "Mama said that once folks moved away, they never came back___except maybe to visit. I might even move to California myself and live next door to you when I get grown."

They were silent, thinking of their separation. Slowly a smile crept across Marlee's face, then erupted in hilarity.

"Benita," she sat up, laughing. "Suppose you decided to move to California at the exact same time that I decided to move back here, and we passed each other on the road. Wouldn't that be funny?" Benita thought so. She sat up too, beside Marlee, only facing her.

"I would be going down the road, and I'd see you coming, and I'd wave at you and shout, 'Hello, Marlee! I hope you enjoy El Paso. I'm going to Los Angeles'. And you'd shout back, 'Hello, Benita! I'm on my way back to El Paso. See you later'."

Both girls rolled on the blanket and laughed and laughed. After a while they grew silent again. "Benita," Marlee said sadly. "Do you think we'll ever see each other again?" "We will, if we promise we will" Benita replied taking her friends hands. "I promise. Cross my heart and hope to die." "Me too. Cross my heart and hope to die." Benita put her arms around Marlee and they hugged each other tight.

At last Marlee pulled away. "As my mama would say, 'no sense in letting tears spoil your day'. Come one, Benita. Lets go sit on your front porch and play jacks."

After Addie left, Vivian packed the lunch basket with the food that her mama had left out for her. Fried chicken, potato salad, hard boiled eggs, a half loaf of Mama's home-made bread and a quarter for soft drinks. She put on the wide-brimmed straw hat to protect her face from the sun, took the basket and her small pocketbook, and walked down to Joshua's house.

Joshua's grandparents, on his daddy's side, lived up in Las Cruses on a farm. At least that's what they called it, with it's one milk cow, a couple dozen chickens, three or four pigs, two mules and old man Dullums's vegetable garden. He was no longer able to work the fields on account of his arthritis, so a neighbor farmer leased the acres and grew cotton. Joshua's daddy - who had died when Josh was eight years old -- and his daddy's only brother, Pete, had been born on the farm, but they both moved to El Paso when they were young men, to work and get married. At least once a month, Uncle Pete drove the forty-some odd miles to see about the old folks. This time Joshua planned to go with his uncle.

When he told Vivian, she came up with a bright idea. "Why don't I pack a lunch for us and ride up to your grandparents with you?" She asked Joshua.

"Really, sweetheart? I'd like that a lot. Are you sure that you won't mind the long ride? There won't be anything for you to do out at grandpa's while Uncle Pete and I do chores for he and grandma." Joshua could hardly contain himself for the joy he felt. To have Vivian with him a whole day -- and it was her suggestion. He knew how much she hated the country. Or anything related to the country, but she was willing to go with him now.

Vivian's reason for going to Las Cruses was not what Joshua thought at all. This was her last chance to spend time with him without feeling that his mama was looking over their shoulder. Mrs. Dullums, a short, skinny woman who probably hadn't grown-

and-inch, or gained-a-pound since she was twelve years old, worked at the hospital at night and slept most of the day.

She was polite and not unfriendly to Vivian, but the two never warmed up to each other. They hadn't had many occasions for conversation since Mrs. Dullums was either sleep or inside when Vivian came to see Joshua. But, there was that one particular time that made Vivian know that she would never be close to Joshua's mama.

Joshua and Vivian had been sitting out back in the swing as they usually did, laughing and talking. They weren't doing anything improper. Just talking, when Mrs. Dullums came out to hang up some clothes.

"Hello, Mrs. Dullums," Vivian said cordially. "Evening, Vivian," The older woman replied in a cool tone. Joshua jumped up to help his mama with the clothes basket, but when he sat the basket under the clothes line he did not return to the swing. Instead he began throwing rocks at a trash can at the back of the yard. Vivian continued to swing. She felt uncomfortable and awkward. Mrs. Dullums hung up two full lines of clothes without saying another word, and all the time Joshua threw rocks. Vivian was relieved when Mrs. Dullums finished, picked up the empty basket, and started for the house.

Just as she came even with Vivian she murmured icily, "Young ladies in my day weren't so brazen when they were trying to attract a young man. What is easily got___ is not usually kept."

She went on into the house, leaving the flabbergasted Vivian with her mouth hanging open. Joshua was too far away to have heard his mother, and besides, he was still throwing rocks at the trash can.

After that incident, Vivian made it a point to avoid the older woman, but she knew from those few words that Joshua's mama was going to be like a "fly in the ointment." That was why she suggested going with Uncle Pete to Las Cruces. Uncle Pete liked her. Furthermore...<u>he</u> didn't think that she was brazen.

She never mentioned the one-way conversation to Joshua. After all, Mrs. Dullums <u>was</u> his mama, and he would never believe that she was capable of being anything but a sweet, hard-working woman who dedicated her life to her son.

When Vivian arrived at the Dullums's house, Uncle Pete was already there. His automobile sat at the curb in front of the house. She let out a big sigh of relief. She wouldn't have to go inside, unless Joshua wasn't ready.   "Please God," She breathed a short prayer. "Let Josh be ready." God must have heard her because Joshua and Uncle Pete came out of the front door just as she put her foot on the bottom step.

The ride up to the country was nice. Hot, but nice. Uncle Pete suggested that they all sit on the front seat, with her in the middle. Almost before they got out of town Joshua casually put his arm on the back of the seat, resting his hand lightly on her shoulder. Uncle Pete seemed not to notice as they bounced along the highway. He and Joshua where engaged in a fervent conversation about cars and motors and things that Vivian didn't understand. Nor did she mind. Right now she was happy just to be sitting beside her Josh.

Grandpa and Grandma Dullums greeted the three travelers warmly, and bid them come inside the old farmhouse for some cold lemonade. "Where did you find such a pretty girl, Josh?" Grandma Dullums asked, busying herself with pouring the cool drinks.

Joshua stammered, embarrassed, "Oh___Granny." Vivian smiled modestly. She was accustomed to hearing folk say that she was pretty.

It was late afternoon when Joshua and Uncle Pete finished all the chores for the old folks. Vivian stayed around the house with Granny - as Grandma Dullums told the young girl to call her - acting domestic. She wanted to win over this part of the family, at least. After supper, the old folks, Uncle Pete, Joshua and Vivian sat out on the porch, telling each other the latest news, swatting flies and drinking more lemonade.

"Why don't you young ones go for a walk," Granny suggested. "You don't want to spend your last few hours together looking in our faces." When Joshua protested, they all laughed uproariously.

"Go on along, boy," Grandpa Dullums urged, winking at his wife. "We understand. We was young once too, wasn't we Mama?" Before Granny Dullums could reply, Joshua took Vivian by the hand and they ran off, across the yard and down the path that led to a small lake behind the house.

The water glistened from the rays of the evening sun as it gradually set in the west. The lake was deserted except for a man in a canoe over on the far shore, anchored among tall reeds. His fishing pole rested in one hand and a can of beer or something was in the other hand as he waited for a fish to bite.

Joshua led Vivian to a sandy spot along the shore where they could sit down. It was where the shore line curved in such a way that the reflection of the lights in Las Cruses could be seen at dark. Joshua stuck his hand into his pocket and withdrew a tiny oblong box. "I wanted to give you something so that you wouldn't forget me," he said, handing the box to Vivian. "Forget you?" she replied passionately. "How in the world could I forget you? I love you, Josh."

"I know. I guess I was just saying something to get you to say what you did." He grinned sheepishly. "Go on, sweetheart. Open it." She lifted the top. "Oh, Josh. It's lovely," she exclaimed happily as she held up the delicate bracelet. There were three gold charms attached to the chain. The letter "J", a heart, and the letter "V". She linked the bracelet around her slender brown wrist and locked the clasp.

"I'll never take it off, Josh. Not ever__except when I bath, but not any other time." She leaned over close to him and kissed him full on the mouth. A deep lingering kiss. They had kissed before, lightly on the mouth or on the cheek___but never like this. Joshua kissed her back.   Then, with a momentary feeling of guilt, drew away as he glanced across the lake, hoping that the fisherman hadn't seen them. The fisherman had gone.

"Does this mean that we're engaged, or something?" Vivian asked with a flirtatious look in her eyes.   "If you want to be, sweetheart," Joshua replied. At that moment he would have agreed to almost anything, he was so content. "Oh, Josh. I'm so happy. I can hardly wait until next summer."

"What's next summer, sweetheart?" He asked absently as he showered her with affectionate kisses on her ear lobes.   "You know, silly," Vivian giggled. "Next summer, when we graduate and you come to L.A., and we get married."

"You're a determined little lady, aren't you?"   Joshua chuckled good naturedly, leaning back to appraise his sweetheart. "You know we aren't getting married until I finish college. And definitely not in Los Angeles." He leaned over to kiss her again, but Vivian drew back.

"But Josh," she pouted. "I thought we had decided not to wait four or five years. And I want to live where my family is. Not___in El Paso."

Joshua took both of her hands and kissed each fingertip. "WE...didn't decide. You got that idea all by yourself." He said, smiling in that charming way of his. "Let's don't talk about marriage and stuff. Let's enjoy ourselves while we have a chance. Who knows, you may not want to marry me after you get out to California and see all those handsome guys out there."

"Joshua Dullums, be serious! Promise me that you will come to L.A. next summer. We can make plans then, alright?" Vivian didn't like the way this conversation was going. She had been sure that Joshua would go her way, but instead he wasn't even taking her seriously. Brushing his hand away she jumped up. "Promise me, Josh, or we'll part as nothing more than friends." He was startled. He tried to put his arms around her but she moved out of his reach and declared vehemently, "I mean it, Josh!"

His heart sank. "I can't make you that kind of promise, sweetheart." *So that's why she wanted to come to the country with me.* "You know that I love you, and I'd do anything in the world for you, that I could. I'm sorry, real sorry, but I'm going to college and I don't ever intend to live in California." He spoke in a low resolute voice. *My mama was right. Vivian is a selfish, self centered girl, and now she is threatening to ruin everything between us because of her selfishness.* "I love you, sweetheart. I imagine I'll always love you, but it has to be the way it has to be."

Vivian moved close to the dejected looking young man, took his face in her hands and caressed him with a tender lingering kiss. Then, dropping her arms, she said with determination, "You're right Josh. It does have to be the way it has to be." Squaring her shoulders in a defiant gesture, she turned and, without looking back, retraced her steps up the path to the farmhouse.

Joshua watched until Vivian was out of sight, picked up a rock and threw it across the lake, his eyes misty as he watched the stone skip across the water.

TRAIN

CHAPTER SEVEN

"The sun has riz, the sun has set, and here we is in Texas yet." Addie thought of the well known phrase describing the vastness of the Lone Star state.

True, the sun was rising and she was in Texas, but by the time that the sun set Addie and her family (except Andy) would be somewhere out in New Mexico. California bound. At last the departure day arrived, as they knew that it must, whether they liked it or not.

Vivian and Addie where the first ones out of bed. A little before daybreak. Addie started a fire in the wood stove for the last time. She cooked oatmeal and skillet toast for breakfast while Vivian curled her thick black hair in the bathroom, running back and forth to heat the curling iron over the fire that blazed up between the half-opened lid on one side of the stove.

One by one the other children woke up. After washing up, they folded and stored their bedclothes and linen in a large box that had been left open, then took their seat at the kitchen table.

Andy said grace over the food as was his custom since the death of his daddy, but this morning it wasn't by rote. This time the prayer was from his heart. "Lord," he prayed in a husky voice. "We thank you for this food we are about to receive for the nourishment of our bodies. And Lord," he paused, then opening his eyes he raised his head toward heaven. His eyes glistened as he continued, "Please, please, bless each one of our family as we go our separate ways. Mama, and Viv, and Jack, and the twins, and don't forget little Ben. Give them a safe trip Lord. And Lord...bless me, too. Keep us together in spirit, while we're absent, one from another. Amen."

It was an emotional moment. The boys ate in silence, but Vivian kept sniffing and Marlee let the tears run down her cheeks unchecked, until the front of her dress was damp. Addie went around the table, kissing and embracing each of her children. Andy had expressed all of their hearts in his short, simple prayer.

After breakfast, the girls helped their mama wash and pack the remaining dishes and cooking utensils, while the boys loaded the truck with everything that was to go on the train. Andy, along with Jack and Mark left as soon as the last box was on the truck, for the train station. Aunt Hettie (the only family member who owned an automobile) would come over in her model-T Ford and drive the rest of them to the depot in plenty of time to see Andy off on the 12:02 for Austin. The train for California was scheduled to leave an hour later, at 1:10.

Ben and Vivian sat on the steps, waiting for Aunt Hettie. Vivian was sure that Joshua would come down the street any minute. She refused to believe that he would let her go without begging her to make-up. *He will realize that I'm right, and come running back,* she thought. So___she sat, waiting.

Addie walked through the house for a final look, with Marlee following close behind, responding to her mama's remarks just like a little old woman. "I'm sure gonna miss this place," Addie murmured, running her hand along the walls as she went, her heart heavy with reminiscence. "Uh-huh. Me too," Marlee replied solemnly.

"Wonder what mama's house is like? I do hope she's got good neighbors." "Uh-huh. Me too." Addie went to the back door and stood looking out into the yard. "Ben's gonna be lost without his pond." "Uh-huh. Sure will be," Marlee stood, with folded arms, beside her mama. "I must say, I'm a little disappointed that none of our neighbors have come over to wish us well," Addie said, more to herself than to her daughter.

Suddenly, from out front, Aunt Hettie blew the horn of her automobile. Addie turned around abruptly, and almost knocked Marlee off of her feet. Grabbing her before she fell, Addie steadied her daughter.

"I'm sorry, baby," she apologized. "Bless your little heart, you're always somewhere near your mama, aren't you?" "Yes, ma'am," Marlee replied soulfully. "That's because I love you, Mama." A pensive expression crossed her face. "Mama, I don't want to move either, but it won't be too bad in Los Angeles so long as we are together, will it?" The small woman and the even smaller girl looked into each others eyes, a deep need to reassure themselves.

"It's gonna be just fine, baby. And I promise you one thing. If I have anything to do with it, you and I are going to come back here one day. I don't know how...or when, but we will. So you just hold on to that thought, you hear me, baby?" "I will, Mama. And I promise, too. We'll come back home, someday."

Vivian had been right about Joshua, who, hot and sweaty, came running through the gate just before Aunt Hettie drove up. "Viv, sweetheart," he panted. "I was scared that I had missed you. I couldn't let you leave without apologizing for last night." Vivian rose from the steps, triumphant, and went to him, throwing her arms around his neck. She didn't care who saw them. Her Joshua

was back. "I forgive you, Josh. You know I love you, don't you?"
"I hope so, sweetheart. I love you."

Her whispered, "I just knew that you would see it my way,"
was drowned out by the, "ah__oooh__gah, ah__oooh__gah" of the
horn on Aunt Hettie's automobile. Joshua jumped back from
Vivian as though he had been shot. He was so embarrassed that he
couldn't look Aunt Hettie in the face when she spoke to him. He
didn't know that she had been so occupied with parking her
automobile that she didn't even notice them embracing. Nor did he
realize that Vivian assumed that his appearance meant that he had
changed his mind about marriage, and California. Worst of all,
Vivian was totally unaware that Joshua had not heard <u>her</u> remark
about "seeing it my way".

It took no more than twenty minutes to drive downtown to
the depot. Ben was so excited with all the activity, and the treat of
riding in Aunt Hettie's car, that for a change he was speechless.
Besides, he had always been a little fearful of Aunt Hettie. Unlike
Addie, Aunt Hettie was stern, and she didn't tolerate foolishness
from young-ones. That's what she called Addie's children. Young-
ones.

Ben wondered why Aunt Hettie was always telling his
mama how she should raise them__especially since Aunt Hettie
didn't have (as Marlee once said) chick, nor child. He didn't think
that Aunt Hettie liked Marlee too much. One time he heard Aunt
Hettie tell Mama that Marlee's fast mouth was going to get her in a
world of trouble one of these days. As Ben climbed into the
automobile and scooted over next to the window, he concluded, *I
guess I'd better enjoy riding in an automobile now. They might not
even have any automobiles out in Los Angeles.*

Andy was standing near the entrance of the depot, waiting to direct Addie and the others to where Mark and Jack were waiting. As they neared the boarding gate Marlee jerked Addie's sleeve and shouted excitedly, "Mama, look! There's Mrs. Johnson, and Mrs. Tate!"

Sure enough it was. Mrs. Johnson was their next door neighbor, and Mrs. Tate lived down at the corner. *What in the world are they doing here?* Addie wondered. Then she grew excited. "OH, MY LORD!" she declared. "Hettie, do you see what I see? Oh, my Lord!" Yes, Hettie saw what she saw. It's was Hettie's idea. All their neighbors, relatives, and even several of the children's teachers, along with the Pastor, where gathered in the depot to wish them farewell. Some one had painted a sign that said, "ADIOS AMIGOS--VAYA CON DIOS" (GOODBY FRIENDS, GO WITH GOD). Most of the adults carried various sized packages. The pastor prayed a loud stirring prayer for the family, right there in the depot. One by one, all of the dear folks hugged Addie, shook Andy's hand, and patted the other children on their shoulder.

Addie was overcome with emotion. She had no idea that she and her family were so loved. Many of the women cried and made Addie promise to write. Finally the boarding call came for Andy's train, so the family went through the gate for their private goodby to him. A porter who had worked with Andy took the food and gifts out to the boarding platform for them. When Addie tried to give him a tip, he simply patted her shoulder. "I should be tipping you," he said. "Your late husband and this young man have been true friends to me." He shook Andy's hand vigorously and walked away.

Now it was Andy's turn to cry. He hugged each of his brothers and sisters, murmuring a few words as he did. When he got to Ben he picked him up and held him close for a long moment.

"You be good, little fellow, and mind Mama." His voice quavered. Ben was his heart. In a vain attempt to console the now crying child, he added with false joviality, "I'll be seeing you again before you have time to miss me. Alright?" "Alright...Andy," Ben sobbed. "I love you, Andy. Did you know...that I love you?" "Come on, baby," Addie said, taking the little boy from Andy and handing him to Jack. She could see that Andy was emotionally spent.

"You better get on the train, son," she sighed. "We'll be just fine. Write me as soon as you get there, and I'll write from grandma's." The mother and son held each other a long time.

"ALLLL ABOARD!" The call came. Andy kissed his mama one last time, waved to the others, and boarded the train.

Less than an hour after Andy left, the west-bound Sunset Limited train pulled out of El Paso, not scheduled to stop until it reached Albuquerque. Once the Halls were settled in their seats, Addie pinned small square pieces of paper on Marlee, Mark and Ben, with their name and Grandma Samuels address on each one. That was in case one of them wandered away and got lost on the train. The chances of that happening were slim because Mark and Marlee were so entranced (or frightened) by the train, and the trip, that they never let go of each others hand___except when one of them had to use the toilet or eat. Ben, who knelt in the seat next to his mama, kept his nose glued to the window. The scenery captured and held his attention, and he only looked away when Addie compelled him to, or he fell asleep.

Jack and Vivian sat next to one another across the aisle from the twins, who were in front of Addie. Jack was so tired that he immediately slumped down in his seat and took a nap.

The people in the coach where the Hall's were riding brought their lunch baskets, or sacks, or boxes of food for their meals. Most were Negroes, and a few Mexicans. They were not allowed to eat in the dining car, but they could pay one of the porters or cooks to bring them food. Addie had enough for her family, and some to spare, so she only bought hot coffee for herself, and cold drinks for the children. That was how she came to meet one of the Negro cooks, and realize that even though she was a widow, she was still young enough to want to be admired.

The train and the evening sun raced to see which one would stay ahead of the other. The sun won as it sank below the horizon, leaving the Sunset Limited to continue into the night. "Good evening, ma'am," said the pullman porter, addressing Addie as he stood, pad and pencil in hand, ready to take her order. "Do you folks care for anything from the dinning car? We have coffee, lemonade, root-beer, coca cola, and sandwiches."

Addie glanced up, somewhat startled. She had been gazing out of the window, into the dusk, into the past. Her mind far, far away. With reluctance she returned to the present. "Yes suh," she replied. "I'd like some hot coffee, and three lemonades. You can ask the girl and boy over there what they want." She gestured toward Vivian and Jack. "Can I order what I want, too?" Ben asked, turning from the window. It was getting too dark outside to hold his attention any longer. "No, baby." "Why, Mama? Why can't I?" "Because you can't, Benjamin," Addie answered through clenched teeth, with finality. Ben gave Addie a puzzled glance. He knew what 'Benjamin' meant. <u>Don't ask again!</u> He slumped down in the seat and stared at his hands. Then, with the sensitivity of a child, he climbed into Addie's lap and hugged her neck. She made no reply, only held him close. She was so tired. For a while she had found comfort in daydreaming about Big Andy, but the porter forced her back to reality. She felt resentful and was taking it out on Ben. Maybe some hot coffee and something to eat would make her feel better.

"Ben, baby," she said, changing her tone. "Go over and tell Vivian to get the picnic basket so we can eat supper." "Alright, Mama," he replied with a wide grin. She kissed him and stood him in the aisle. He had been in his seat for the last several hours, and it felt good to walk around. The swaying motion of the train made him giggle as he made his way across the aisle to his sister's seat.

"Viv! Viv!" he almost screamed. "Mama said to get the picnic basket down." "I'm not deaf, Ben." Vivian muttered, pulling the boy close. "Do you always have to talk so loud?" He wrenched away from her and made haste to scramble across Addie to the safety of his seat as Vivian took the basket from an overhead rack. Handing it to her mama she asked, "Why didn't you have Jack get this? You knew Ben would let everybody on this train know my name."

Addie answered wearily, "Because you were sitting on the aisle and it was easier for you to reach the basket. Besides, I don't think everybody__or anybody, for that matter__cares what your name is." "Oh Mama," Vivian pursed her mouth and rolled her eyes with disgust. "You don't understand what I mean." "No, I guess I don't." *Vivian, Vivian, Vivian,* Addie sighed to herself. *When are you going to learn that the world don't revolve around you?* "Why don't you make yourself useful and help me with this food, darling," Addie said in her sweetest voice.

By the time that everyone had their supper on paper plates firmly settled on their laps, the drinks arrived. A tall, light-skinned fortyish looking man carried the order on a tray. "I have your order, ma'am," he said.

Vivian leaned around her seat to see where the voice was coming from, then whispered to Jack, "He sounds like Daddy, doesn't he?" "No!" Was his emphatic reply. "Yes he does," Vivian insisted. Jack busied himself with his food, ignoring her, all the while straining to hear what his mama and the man were saying.

"You're not the same porter who took my order, are you?" Addie asked, knowing full well that he wasn't. She too had noticed how much he sounded like Big Andy. "No ma'am," he said as he gave her the tray. "I'm not a porter. I'm a cook." He seemed to be very proud of the fact. "The porter got busy with some other orders, so I offered to bring yours." "That was kind of you." Addie smiled. "My name is Thomas. If you need anything else, just anything...don't hesitate to ask." He grinned, showing a mouth full of gold-plated teeth. Addie made no reply, only nodded her head and turned her attention back to her food. Thomas bowed slightly and left.

Vivian went over to Addie's seat and whispered something in her ear. The two women laughed softly while Jack attacked his food and seethed inside. *What did this stranger mean_telling Mama his name!* Jack thought angrily. *Who cares what his name is? Certainly not Mama.* When Vivian returned to her seat, Jack spoke with sarcasm. "Did you hear that porter?" He asked. "He was getting mighty familiar with Mama."

Vivian gave her brother an impatient frown. "He's not a porter. He's a cook." "Cook___Porter. Who cares? Same difference." "You take things too serious," she said. "The man was just being friendly." "Well, he can go be friendly with somebody else. Not with Mama." Jack squinted his angry dark eyes and stared out of the window.

The next morning Addie's order was taken and returned by the porter. She wouldn't admit it to anyone but herself, but she enjoyed the small amount of attention paid to her by Thomas. And, she liked hearing his voice. So much like Big Andy's. It wasn't until the following day that Thomas appeared again. They were in California now. The desert had given way to high Palm trees and Date groves. Soon they would reach their destination. Ben was in his favorite pose, on his knees with his face glued to the window.

"Hello again," Thomas said, stopping beside Addie's seat on his way to one of the forward coaches. "Hello, ah__Thomas," Addie greeted him, smiling. "Are you going to L.A.?" he asked.

"Yes, we are." "Have you ever been there before?" "No, we haven't. This is our first time." *Why do I keep saying "we"*, she wondered. "My mother lives there." "What part of the city does she live in? I may know her. I've lived in L.A. all my life." Thomas shifted his feet, leaning ever so slightly toward Addie. The tone of his voice intimate. "We might__run into each other while you're there." Addie became uneasy. She wasn't sure whether he was flirting with her, or just being friendly. Anyway, the conversation was going in a direction that was not to her liking. She didn't want to be friends with Thomas. Only hear his voice. Or so she thought.

"I don't know what part of town she lives in. I've never been there before, remember?" she replied, her voice stiff. "That's right. You did say that, didn't you?" He replied in an equally stiff tone. He had been attracted to the extremely beautiful small brown-skinned woman when he first glimpsed her boarding the train. It was no accident when he brought her order night before last. She seemed attracted to him too, then. Now, abruptly, she turned him off, for some reason or other. Bowing politely, he said,

"Well, you'll be in L.A. soon. I hope you enjoy your visit. It was nice talking to you. Goodby and good luck to <u>you all</u>."

Addie hovered between relief, and disappointment as she watched him continue through the coach. As soon as Thomas disappeared through the door, Vivian went over and knelt beside her mama's seat. "What were you all talking about, Mama?" She inquired, grinning. "He is <u>sooo</u> good looking. Did he ask you your name?" "Vivian! I do declare. He was just being friendly, that's all." Addie felt embarrassed__and chagrined__and guilty. "I saw the way he was looking at you," Vivian whispered, slyly. "I wish he had looked my way, even if he is as old as Daddy." "<u>That's enough</u>, young lady. Your daddy hasn't been dead a year. I wouldn't look twice at another man. What kind of woman do you take me for?" Vivian was taken aback. She hadn't meant any harm. "I'm sorry, Mama. I was only teasing." Her eyes implored Addie. "Mama. Forgive me?"

Addie put her arm around the girl's shoulder. "No, you forgive me," she said, a pained expression on her face. "I'm the guilty one. I guess I really did enjoy his attention, and I hate to admit it. Not him in particular, but a male. Really, it was his voice...so much like your daddy's."   "I understand, Mama." Looking at her daughter, she saw for the first time, not a girl anymore, but a woman. A woman who might be able to understand what she was experiencing. She had to confide in somebody to let out some of the loneliness.

"Maybe you do. Maybe you don't. I can't say that I understand myself. But you know what Viv? For a minute there...I felt like a woman again. Like when Big Andy was alive. Viv, do you suppose I'll ever get over missing your daddy so fierce?" "You will, Mama. Like you always told us___it just takes time." Kissing her mama on the cheek, she rose to return to her seat, but couldn't resist a final, "I still say___the man is sooo good looking!" Vivian dodged Addie's hand as the porter came through. "NEXT STOP____LOS ANGELES. END OF THE LINE."

THE END